T0327829

THE KEW GARDENER'S GUIDE TO

GROWING
TREES

THE KEW GARDENER'S GUIDE TO

GROWING
TREES

THE ART AND SCIENCE TO
GROW WITH CONFIDENCE

TONY KIRKHAM

FRANCES
LINCOLN

Contents

Introduction to growing trees

—

THE VALUE OF TREES

Trees in our landscape, whether urban or rural, are often taken for granted by us all and it's not until they are removed and disappear that we realize their significance and the important role that they play in our everyday lives. They are the green infrastructure that bonds our lives together subconsciously, providing a visual, green impact in any season, often breaking up the hard, straight-edged structures of buildings and softening the visual landscape with their sheer presence by their contrasting colours and textures. In a woodland, park or garden, large or small trees generate a feeling of maturity, shade, privacy and stately permanence more than any other plants are able to (see also Researching and finding an old veteran tree, page 124, and Measuring a tree's height and ageing it, page 116). Besides their sheer beauty and elegance, trees actually give a whole range of benefits which affect the wider environment and help to improve our own cultural and spiritual needs, enhancing our physical and mental well-being and reducing daily stress in our lives.

Take the average mature, healthy, hundred-year-old oak tree, which will have approximately 100,000 leaves in its crown. If laid side by side, its leaves will cover an area roughly the size of a football pitch. On an average summer's day, these leaves will absorb around 9kg/20lb of carbon dioxide from the atmosphere, the root system will have drawn 200–400 litres/44–88 gallons of water, which will evaporate from the leaves, and through a process called photosynthesis will produce around 7kg/15lb of oxygen as a waste product – enough to support a family of five people. While carrying out this operation, the leaves will also have filtered out any harmful substances like greenhouse gases and pollutants, bacteria, fungal spores and dust. In addition, the dense leafy canopy will reduce noise pollution, provide shade and ultraviolet (UV) protection during hot sunny days and act as a natural air-conditioning unit by cooling the air through transpiration, which is the evaporation of water through the leaves. By absorbing water via the roots, trees can capture rainfall, reducing the risk of flooding, and can prevent soil erosion by slowing down water run-off following heavy rains.

However, despite all these amazing benefits I would suggest that the main reason why we plant trees in our garden

Spring colour can be just as good as autumn colour, and the golden leaves of the Japanese maple *Acer shirasawanum* 'Jordan' in late spring will brighten up any part of the garden.

is for some form of privacy and for their sheer elegance and ornamental beauty. The many attributes that trees provide include their various shapes and form, their foliage, flowers, fruit and bark – all of which will change with the seasons and from year to year. I hope that this guide will help you to choose, plant and look after the perfect tree.

TREES IN THE GARDEN

There is a place in every garden for a tree, but be sure to think about what you are planting and where, and plant responsibly. Why do you want to plant a tree in the garden is the first question that you should be asking before you think about where to plant it and what species you will choose. Do you want to plant for privacy, as a single ornamental specimen in the lawn or in a border for seasonal interest or to attract wildlife?

For privacy planting, there may be a neighbouring property, windows, ugly street furniture or a busy road that you want to hide. Don't be tempted to plant the old-fashioned conifer hedge (× *Cuprocyparis leylandii*/Leyland cypress) because it is fast-growing and cheap to buy, as in the long term it will potentially become problematic and ugly. It can be the rottweiler of the tree world, get too tall and broad, need regular pruning and eventually, after continuous hard pruning, the woody branches become exposed with no greenery left. It is also a veracious feeder, drying the soil out and shading the rest of the garden, resulting in little else being able to grow anywhere.

It is important to plant a tree in a position that doesn't block out too much light from the rest of the garden, while still giving the desired privacy. Think about the overall height and spread when it's mature. Try to choose one or two suitably sized trees for the size of your garden and plant them at regular or irregular intervals along the boundary to screen it while offering more interest and minimal future maintenance. However, don't plant too close to the neighbour's boundary fence so that the branches won't invade their air space later when the tree grows and the neighbours need to start removing branches from it, unbalancing and spoiling the shape and weakening the tree.

For an ornamental specimen, take your time to choose the best site in the garden where you can view and enjoy the tree without it blocking important sightlines or vistas or interfering with other parts of the garden. Ensure it's not too close to the house to cause problems in the future, too (see How far can you plant a tree from the house?, page 14). For more ideas, see Five hardworking trees for any small garden, page 78.

Planting trees for wildlife can be extremely rewarding. Generally, such trees are native and can produce lots of fleshy fruits such as on rowan (*Sorbus aucuparia*), common hawthorn (*Crataegus monogyna*) and wild cherry (*Prunus avium*), which when eaten by birds are then passed through and deposited, causing a nuisance and possible damage. Thus be sure to plant such trees away from patios, windows, private drives or parking spaces. Another way to attract birds, mammals and invertebrates to your garden is to build an ecological log stack (see page 70) and to provide a bee hotel (see Making a bee hotel, page 94).

Do trees talk to each other?

We have all had the occasional conversation with a tree as we walk through a garden or a woodland, as it's good for our mental well-being, often makes us feel better and trees never answer back. But do trees actually talk to each other? We need to go back to where trees come from in nature: more often than not, trees grow in woodlands or forests and very rarely as solitary specimens. We know that woodlands are communities that are connected to each other by what has been called the 'wood-wide web', an underground network of fungal interaction called mycorrhizae, forming a symbiotic relationship between the fungi and the tree. The mycorrhizae enable the exchange of nutrients and sugars and help to protect the weaker trees from drought, while at the same time swapping information, even between different tree species, and building resilience in the landscape against invasion from pests and diseases, in return simply for a host to live on. Trees do communicate with each other by emitting pheromones, ethylene and other scent-based signals into the air signalling distress. Once these gases are detected through the tree's leaves, each tree can take appropriate steps to protect itself, and in many trees that means increasing tannin levels to make the once-juicy, tender leaves unpalatable. I suppose, talking through smells. So yes, trees do talk to each other, but just not in the same way as you and I.

WHAT IS A TREE?

It may seem obvious what a tree is, yet often there is some confusion between a large shrub like a holly (*Ilex*) or hazel (*Corylus*), which can also be classed as a 'tree', and a small tree like a Japanese maple (*Acer palmatum*), but botanically speaking a tree is a long-lived perennial plant with a permanent woody stem or trunk covered in coarse bark and supporting branches (the scaffold), which split into secondary branches, forming a crown and bearing leaves. The trunk and the branches increase in length and girth each year by making annual rings – a process known as secondary thickening. Below the ground, the trunk and crown are anchored by a root system (see page 13).

Basically, there are two types of trees: **broadleaves**, sometimes known as hardwoods; and **conifers**, which are commonly known as softwoods, both of which can be **evergreen** (retaining their leaves through the winter) or **deciduous** (losing their leaves during autumn and through winter). An example of a deciduous broadleaf is the English oak (*Quercus robur*) and an evergreen broadleaf is the holm oak (*Q. ilex*). An example of an evergreen conifer is the Scots pine (*Pinus sylvestris*) and a deciduous conifer is the European larch (*Larix decidua*).

TREE FORMS AND CROWN SHAPES

No two trees grow alike, even if they are the same species, because they are living dynamic plants whose growth can be affected by differing soil types, local climatic conditions (including rain, wind and light levels) and varying environmental factors (such as pollution, space and human activity). However, trees do come in a variety of shapes and sizes, which are determined by the tree's natural habit. Therefore, knowing the habit of a species or cultivar will help when selecting a suitable tree for a particular space in the garden: for example, if planting in a restricted space it will be more appropriate to select a columnar tree (upright) than a tree with a spreading crown.

Tree crown shapes include rounded, spreading, oval, pyramidal, conical, vase, columnar or fastigiate, open and weeping.

PARTS OF A TREE

It is important to understand the terminology of the various parts of a tree in order to appreciate how a tree grows, when deciding if there is a place in the garden for a specific species of tree. These parts and definitions are set out below.

Roots and root plate

The roots are the main support system for the tree and will develop in size, depth and spread as the tree grows, in order to anchor it in the ground. They are also used by the tree to absorb water and nutrients and to store energy. The network of roots found within the upper 1m/3ft layer of soil is called the root plate and is not a mirror image of the upper part of the tree, which is what we are often incorrectly led to believe.

Root crown

The place where the roots join the trunk or main stem is called the root crown or root collar, and in mature trees this zone will be flared or buttressed.

Trunk

The main purpose of the trunk – or bole as it is also known – is to support the upper parts of the tree towards the sunlight and in nature to compete against other trees in a woodland situation. It is also used to transport water and nutrients from the roots to the tree crown and to distribute food from the leaves to all other parts of the tree.

Bark

The outer layer of the trunk is called bark, and it provides a layer of waterproof tissue to protect the tree against inclement weather, invasion from pests, diseases and animal attack. Bark can be smooth, deeply fissured, flaky, plate-like, papery or even spiny.

Ornamental bark on: (top left) *Prunus serrula*, (top right) *Castanea sativa*, (bottom left) *Acer griseum* and (bottom right) *Arbutus menziesii*.

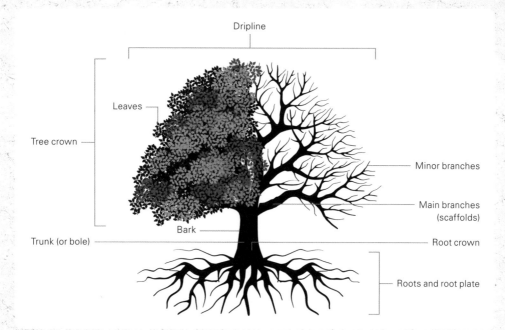

Dripline

Leaves

Tree crown

Minor branches

Main branches
(scaffolds)

Trunk (or bole)

Bark

Root crown

Roots and root plate

These are the different parts of a tree.

Rounded

Spreading

Pyramidal

Oval

Conical

Vase

Columnar

Open

Weeping

These are some of the various forms and crown shapes of trees.

Scaffold

This is the main branch system of the tree that forms the framework for the tree crown. The minor branches bearing the leaves, flowers and fruits are produced from the scaffold.

Tree crown

This is the upper part of the tree growing from the trunk and is made up of the scaffold and the minor branching system supporting the leaf mass, also known as foliage. The outer edge of the crown is called the dripline, as this is generally the wettest part of the tree, where the rainwater drips off the crown.

Leaves

The leaves (foliage) on a tree are its workhorse and are mostly green during the growing season due to the compound chlorophyl, which is used in the process of photosynthesis to convert sunlight and carbon dioxide into energy and oxygen. However, in autumn the weaker pigments in the leaves – the carotins and anthocyanins – are revealed by the withdrawal of green chlorophyll from the leaves (see Making a collage of autumnal leaves in a picture frame, page 50).

How far can you plant a tree from the house?

The general rule of thumb is to work out what the overall height of the tree is when mature and plant it three-quarters of its height away from the house. So, a large tree such as an English oak (*Quercus robur*), which will grow to 30m/100ft high, should be planted no closer than 22m/72ft away from the property. A smaller tree such as a birch (*Betula*), cherry (*Prunus*) or rowan (*Sorbus*) can be planted closer because the roots are less likely to cause any damage to the fabric or foundations of the house. Avoid planting directly on top of underground services like power cables, gas pipes, water pipes and other utilities, because in the future these may need excavation to repair, and the established or mature tree may need to have its roots cut off, ultimately damaging your investment.

These two trees (*Acer griseum* and *Betula nigra* Heritage) are suitable for a small to medium-sized garden but keep away from any building.

Generally speaking, small trees rarely do damage to property unless they fall down, potentially causing some minor physical damage.

FOLIAGE ON BROADLEAVED TREES

This can be arranged in a whorl on a twig (such as on *Catalpa*), alternately along the twig (such as on beech/ *Fagus*) or in pairs opposite each other (such as on maple/*Acer*). In winter, the dormant leaf buds will also be a helpful clue when identifying a tree. Leaves come in a variety of shapes, but we can recognize them by categorizing them into two distinct types: simple and compound.

Simple leaf
A simple leaf is literally a single leaf or blade, with no division, attached to the twig by a petiole (also known as a leaf stalk). The edges or leaf margins can be smooth (or entire), serrated with teeth, lobed, parted or palmate.

- Smooth/entire leaf – beech (*Fagus*)
- Serrated leaf margin – birch (*Betula*) or hornbeam (*Carpinus*)
- Lobed leaf – English oak (*Quercus robur*) or Spanish oak (*Q. pyrenaica*)
- Parted leaf – red oak (*Q. rubra*) or shumard oak (*Q. shumardii*)
- Palmate – maple (*Acer*) or sweetgum (*Liquidambar styraciflua*)

Compound leaf
This is made up of several single leaf blades or leaflets, which are all attached to a main central petiole by their own short petioles. The leaf margins can be smooth or serrated.

- Pinnate – rowan (*Sorbus*)
- Trifoliate – paperbark maple (*Acer griseum*)
- Compound palmate – Indian horse chestnut (*Aesculus indica*)

Smooth/entire leaf
Fagus x taurica

Serrated leaf margin
Carpinus betulus

Lobed leaf
Quercus pyrenaica

Parted leaf
Quercus shumardii

Palmate
Acer forrestii

Pinnate
Sorbus commixta

Trifoliate
Acer griseum

Compound palmate
Aesculus indica

FOLIAGE ON CONIFERS

The leaves of most conifers are designed to survive in harsh weather such a drought, wind, snow and cold. They can be long and narrow (and known as needles) or flat, triangular and scale-like – both shapes having a waxy surface and stomatal pores, which are used for breathing and are set in hidden grooves. The different types can be categorized into four.

Awl-like leaves
These conifer leaves resemble mini teeth and are made up of lots of small needles stacked on top of one another.

- Japanese redwood (*Cryptomeria japonica*)

Linear leaves
Flattened leaves rather than rounded needles are attached along the twigs.

- The true silver firs, Nordmann fir (*Abies nordmanniana*)
- Douglas fir (*Pseudotsuga menziesii*)
- The hemlocks, Western hemlock (*Tsuga heterophylla*)

Needles
These conifer leaves are green, occasionally with a glaucous-blue sheen, long, thin, round and in bundles or clusters.

- In bundles of 2, 3 or 5, the pines, Scot's pine (*Pinus sylvestris*)
- In clusters of 15 to 35 needles along the twig, the true cedars, cedar of Lebanon (*Cedrus libani*)
- Singly along the twigs, the spruces, Norway spruce (*Picea abies*)

Scale-like leaves
Also known as random-leaved, these conifer needles are mini branches covered in scales.

- Juniper (*Juniperus communis*), arborvitae (*Thuja plicata*) or cypresses (*Cupressus sempervirens*)

Awl-like leaf
Cryptomeria japonica

Linear leaf
Abies nordmanniana

Linear leaf
Pseudotsuga menziesii

Linear leaf
Tsuga heterophylla

Needles
Pinus sylvestris

Needles
Cedrus libani

Needles
Picea abies

Scale-like leaf
Thuja plicata

It is important to plant the right-sized tree in the right space. Here are newly planted Yoshino cherries (*Prunus* x *yedoensis*).

PLANTING THE RIGHT TREE IN THE RIGHT PLACE

Planting a tree is a long-term investment, and it is extremely important, after planting and once established in its new home, that the tree will be around for many years to give you and future generations much enjoyment and pleasure. Therefore, it is important to plant the right tree in the right place, allowing it to grow to its potential size and shape without any major interference. Space in the garden will be the main limiting factor for choice, so opt for a spot where the tree will not shade the house nor cause any physical damage to foundations (see also Trees in the garden, page 10, and How far can you plant a tree from the house?, page 14). Stand in the proposed planting site and pretend that you are the mature tree. Look around you for 360 degrees and imagine what space you will need as you grow; spread your arms like the tree's branches and check for anything above the ground like structures and cables that may get in the way of the tree's upright and spreading growth and development.

Assessing the site and soil conditions
A key part of successfully establishing a tree is finding the right tree for the soil conditions in your garden, so it is

In the drier part of a garden, a Judas tree (*Cercis siliquastrum*) makes a stunning sight in spring before its leaves appear.

very important to know what soil type is present where you are thinking of planting the tree. An easy way to do this is to look around in neighbouring gardens, parks and woodlands and observe what are the most common species growing, while at the same time assessing whether they are looking healthy. Then choose a species that is closely related or with similar traits.

Most soils in our gardens are very artificial, made up of years of cultivation usually by improving soil condition with the addition of compost and fertilizer. However, they may also be compacted, lacking any form of structure, nutrients and organic matter,

due to an absence of cultivation. Do a quick test to check the soil type by touching and rolling it around in your hand to determine if it is sandy, clay or silty soil and what conditioning it will need to grow certain trees (see individual tree profiles, pages 46–129). Another important aspect is the pH (whether the soil is acid or alkaline). Use of a simple DIY kit available in most garden centres will quickly tell you the relevant acidity or alkalinity, which will help you identify what trees you will and will not be able to grow without continuous soil amelioration work.

Exposure to sunlight and wind will also play a role in tree selection.

The various sizes and forms of trees that can be bought

Transplants and whips – transplants are small broadleaved trees or conifers, usually 3–4 years old and used for planting windbreaks, woodlands and hedges. Whips are taller broadleaved transplants with no lateral branches on the stem.
Maidens – young, single-stemmed trees about a finger thick and up to 1.2m/4ft tall; they are one year old and may have lateral branches. Young fruit trees and ornamental cultivars, which are grafted, are often sold in this category.
Feathered trees – single-trunk trees with lateral branches making a skirt from ground level to the growing point.
Standard trees – trees each with a single, upright, clean trunk (to any height) and a well-balanced crown with a clear leader or a uniform, well-trained, branched crown. See also Creating a standard topiary ball, page 110.
Multi-stemmed trees – trees with more than one dominant trunk, usually three to five, which are created in the nursery by coppicing (see page 41).

Transplant

Whip

Maiden

Feathered

Standard

Multi-stemmed

Most will need full sun, and some will do well in partial shade, but few will perform well in deep shade. Wind will determine where trees are planted and staked (see also Tree staking, page 26). It can also dry out soils, causing drought conditions, as well as physically damage branches during storms.

Hardiness
This is the tree's ability to survive in extreme temperatures, from winter cold to summer highs. In this guide we provide a reference to the hardiness of the trees described, using the system introduced by the Royal Horticultural Society (RHS). This has seven main categories of temperature ranges: from zone 1 for greenhouse plants to zone 7 for plants that are totally hardy. Therefore, before you make your final choice of tree, find out the zone rating that you are in and make sure the plant that you select is hardy in your area.

Choosing a tree
Selecting the type of tree to plant should be enjoyable, and in the end is your personal choice. There is a suitable tree for every situation so, having estimated the maximum size that the space can accommodate and the conditions in the potential site, you can then go deeper into the tree's ornamental attributes.

Trees have many features that we can enjoy through the seasons: for example, the leaf size, shape and colour; flowers; fruits; and bark. Some trees tick more than one of these boxes, giving us aesthetic pleasure each season, and they certainly justify their position in the garden (see Five hardworking trees for any small garden, page 78).

BUYING A TREE

There are various ways to procure a tree (nursery stock), but the best way to ensure that you get what you want – a fine healthy specimen – is to visit a retail nursery or garden centre, look at the trees for yourself and choose the very tree that you are buying, so that you know what you are getting. Most retail outlets will welcome this approach, will encourage you to do so and will give you any advice that is needed.

Where trees are sold online, the nurseryman will usually, if asked, send you a photograph of the actual tree growing on the nursery, which will help you to make your choice.

I am a fan of nursery visits, self-selection and tagging it myself, especially if it is of large nursery stock, and this should be an exciting part of the tree planting process. That said, you still must not be deterred from buying online or by mail order, and there are many nurseries that sell trees online, providing good descriptions and a competitive delivery service.

Biosecurity
One of the biggest threats to our trees is the introduction of exotic pests and diseases from overseas, which can potentially destroy populations of trees and have a devastating effect on the native treescape: for example, ash dieback (see page 133) and Dutch elm disease. To reduce this risk, you must aim to buy locally sourced and grown trees from nearby reputable nurseries.

When returning from a holiday abroad, do not be tempted to bring back seeds or cuttings of trees as you could be introducing a new tree pest or disease.

Three root types are available when buying a tree: (left) root-balled, (top right) container-grown and (bottom right) bare-root.

Nursery stock

There are various types and sizes of nursery stock available, from small transplants to semi-mature specimens, (see page 19) in a range of forms and prices, but all of them will have started their life on and been grown in a tree nursery. The size and age of the tree that you are looking to buy will determine what type of root system is on the tree. These can be:

Bare-root, meaning that there is no soil attached to the root system and the roots are exposed and clean. Whenever a bare-root tree is bought, it should come root-wrapped with some form of protection around the roots such as a poly-planting bag to keep them moist and stop them drying out. These are usually the cheapest trees to buy.

Root-balled, which is where a tree is lifted directly from the nursery field, together with its roots inside a ball of soil. This ball will be wrapped in hessian with chicken wire around the root ball to prevent it falling apart during transit.

Container-grown, which means exactly what it says: the tree has been grown in a container with compost for at least a full growing season. The container can be a variety of types from rigid black plastic plant pots to specialist white bags and special, recycled-plastic, perforated pots that air prune the roots as they reach the wall of each container.

Containerized. There is a difference between container-grown and containerized trees. Containerized trees are those trees that have been potted up and sold before they have had a chance to root into the compost. Often bare-root trees that have not been sold before the end of the planting season are potted up to extend the sale period, but when knocked out of the pot they become bare-root trees again. A good example of a containerized tree is when a Christmas tree is dug up from the field and planted temporarily in a container for the Christmas period; thus, the tree has not been grown in the container for very long. Why not grow your own Christmas tree in a container and bring it in the house each Christmas (see Grow your own Christmas tree, page 84).

LOOKING AFTER A TREE BETWEEN BUYING AND PLANTING

Trees are living things and should be treated so. Once the tree has been chosen and purchased it is important to be sure that it can be easily handled and transported to the planting site. If it is too large for a car, make local arrangements for the nursery or garden centre to deliver it. During transit, the tree's root system, trunk and branches should be protected to avoid any possible damage, especially from any rubbing of the bark on sharp angles.

Storing the tree between buying and planting
The sooner the tree is planted after delivery the better. Meanwhile, always store the tree in a safe, windproof, temporary position outdoors, ensuring that the roots are protected and not allowed to dry out. This can be done by 'heeling in' bare-root trees. First dig a small trench and place the soil along one side of the trench, creating a low bank. Take the roots out of the protective covering or bag and place them in the open trench with the upper part of the trees leaning at an angle against the soil banked along the side of the trench. Cover the roots in the trench with friable soil, creating a slight mound and ensuring that no roots are exposed or sticking out of the trench. Water in and do not allow the soil to dry out. By temporarily heeling in the tree you will gain time in the dormant season to finalize a permanent position in the garden in which to plant the tree.

If the tree is growing in a container or is root-balled, there will be plenty of soil around its roots, which will provide some form of protection provided its soil is kept moist until planting time.

Tree care tips

Always:
- Carry the tree by the root system or the container; never by the trunk.
- Store the tree upright if it is in a pot or root-balled.
- Treat the tree as a living thing, so give it air, light and water during storage.

Never:
- Drop the tree from a height.
- Store a tree in a warm building.
- Allow the roots or top to dry out.

A good way to store bare-root trees temporarily is to heel them into a trench in the garden – here (above) Douglas fir (*Pseudotsuga menziesii*) and (left) hazel (*Corylus avellana*). This will protect the roots until the trees can be planted in their permanent positions.

PLANTING A TREE

When it comes to putting a tree in the ground, every site, soil and position in the garden will vary, so each tree will most likely be planted with a different approach. However, there are several principles to follow when doing so, which will lead to a healthy tree and successful establishment.

> *The best time to plant a tree was 20 years ago; the second-best time is now.*
>
> (Chinese proverb)

Optimum time

What time of the year or season is the best one to plant a tree? Providing it is followed up by aftercare, planting can be done at any time of year. However, the ideal times are in autumn through the winter into early spring. I prefer an autumn planting as the roots will continue to grow and establish well into the winter period when the tree top is dormant.

Equipment

It is important to have the right tools at hand to do the job properly:

- spade;
- fork;
- half-moon turfing iron (when planting in a lawn);
- string;
- stout bamboo cane or length of wood;
- a pair of good-quality, sharp secateurs.

Preparing and placing

We will imagine that we are planting a tree into a lawn but the general principles can be applied to any other site. Attach a piece of long string to a central point where the tree will be positioned and mark out a circle with a diameter of 1.5m/5ft or more. Strip, remove and dispose of the turf to expose the soil surface. Within the circle, mark out a square and dig out the soil to the length of a spade blade (28cm/11in) or to the depth of the root system on the tree if that is greater. Remove the container from the tree and check that there are no circling roots. If there are, tease them out or cut them off with secateurs to stop them from continuing to circle.

Place the tree in the centre of the planting hole with the nursery mark (where the trunk met the soil when the tree was growing in the container) level with the surrounding turf or, if in a flower bed, with the surrounding soil surface. Check from all angles that the tree is straight and not leaning, and then backfill with the soil that was removed from the hole, doing so in layers and firming with the foot as you go. Put back as much as you need of the soil until the correct level is achieved. It is not necessary to enrich the soil with any additives such as compost or fertilizer, as these are not needed by a newly planted tree.

When finished, the top of the root ball should still be visible at the base of the tree trunk. Then add an organic mulch to a depth of 10cm/4in around the base of the trunk, covering all the soil surface of the planting hole but ensuring the mulch does not touch the trunk (see also Mulching trees, page 29). This will prevent any competition from weed

Within the turf circle, dig out a square hole to the depth of the spade blade.

Position the tree in the centre of the hole with the nursery mark level with the surrounding turf.

Backfill the hole with the soil that came out, firming it as you go.

Mulch the soil surface with an organic mulch, leaving a 'doughnut' space around the base of the tree.

Key principles when tree planting

- use suitable tools for the job;
- dig a square shallow planting hole to the depth of the root system;
- position the tree at the correct depth in the centre of the hole;
- backfill the soil without additives and firm in layers;
- apply organic mulch to the surface of the planting hole around the tree.

growth and minimize evaporation of water in the soil, thereby reducing the amount of watering needed. Water well after mulching; as well as helping the tree establish, this will stop the soil capping and will bed in the mulch. Finally check if there are any branches that have been damaged or broken between buying and planting, and remove these with sharp secateurs.

TREE STAKING

Not every tree planted will require a support, especially if it is sited in a sheltered position in a garden. However, some form of tree staking may be needed if the tree is large or tall and its root system is small or lacks a weighty root ball to balance the top, or if the site is constantly subjected to strong winds. Every tree and site should be assessed individually, and then the question asked: 'To stake or not to stake?' Do not stake for the sake of staking.

If the tree is relatively small with a thin bendy trunk, a stout garden cane will often suffice. Push the cane into the ground beside the planted tree and secure it to the tree using a suitable tying material that will not cut into the thin bark on the trunk and will expand as the tree trunk grows. Tie it in a figure of eight, ensuring there is the width of a hand on edge between the tree and its support.

A larger tree will require some support from a tree stake (round timber), which should be positioned on the prevailing wind side of the tree. When banging it into the ground bear in mind that it will need to be removed at some time within the next two years so don't insert it so deep that it will moor the QE2 ship. Think about the size of tree the stake will be supporting.

There are various methods of staking a tree, but, as with planting a tree, if you follow some basic principles, success should be the result.

The most common way to support a tree is with a single stake, the top of which should be one-third of the overall height of the tree. This is where the tree will be attached to the stake with a single proprietary tree tie and buffer. Never use string, wire, electrical cable ties or tights.

If a tree with a root ball has been planted and it is impossible to insert the stake without damaging the tree roots, the same principle can be adopted using two stakes and a cross bar or else a stake angled at 45 degrees (oblique). The tree is then attached at the same point (one-third of the overall height of the tree) using a tree tie or tree-tie material. See also Checking supports, page 30.

There are three suitable methods of staking trees following planting: for bare-root trees (top left) use a single stake; for a root-balled tree (top right) insert an oblique stake or (bottom left) fix two stakes and a cross bar. All the stakes should be attached to the tree at one-third of the overall height of the tree.

Watering trees is very important after planting, especially during dry weather. Here a Japanese maple (*Acer palmatum*) is steadily watered until the soil is wet deep down at root level.

This 'tree watering bag' can be filled with water, which will slowly percolate over a ten-hour period through the fine stitching in the bottom of the bag, putting the water where it is needed.

AFTERCARE FOLLOWING PLANTING

This is so important in order to get the tree to independence, but it is often overlooked or neglected. However, if you can spare just a little time to give some aftercare, it will certainly pay off by encouraging a healthy tree.

Protection

Depending on the situation, it may be necessary to provide some form of protection for the tree from animals. This can be in the form of a wire cage or a proprietary spiral tree guard. Any form of guard should be checked at regular intervals to ensure it is still providing some protection and is not damaging the tree.

Watering trees

One of the main reasons why newly planted trees fail to establish and so die is due to lack of water, especially during dry periods in spring and summer. During the early years of a tree's life, drought is detrimental to its health and vigour (see also page 136). It is difficult to prescribe exactly how much water should be applied, but the general rule should be to check the moisture in the soil underneath the mulch to the depth of the roots, and if it's too dry it will need watering.

To ensure that any water given to the tree is not lost to evaporation or drying winds, a good layer of mulch will also help to stop weeds from competing for the nutrients and water.

Mulching trees

There are various types of mulch that can used around the bases of trees following planting, including proprietary mulch mats made from organic and non-organic materials. I prefer a good clean organic matter such as garden compost, composted horse manure, composted bark or woodchips, which can be taken down into the soil under the tree as the organic matter breaks down naturally and is used as an organic feed by the tree, as and when it needs it. This will also reduce the amount of water needed by the young tree during its early stages of growth and establishment and will prevent competitive weeds from growing around the base of the tree.

The organic mulch must be kept topped up to 10cm/4in deep, with a clear area like a 'doughnut' around the base of the tree. It is important not to let the mulch build up against the trunk base, as this can cause damage by potentially rotting the bark, girdling the trunk and leaving the tree exposed to invasion from wood-rotting fungi.

Weed control

The best means of removing weeds around the tree is by hand-pulling them. If the ground was well prepared before planting, the weeds will pull out easily without too much soil disturbance. If weedkillers are used, some can be absorbed by tree roots exposed on the surface and can cause permanent damage to the tree.

Do not use a strimmer near a young tree as the cord can bruise the bark and girdle the trunk if it comes into contact, and so will ultimately kill the tree.

Feeding
Most newly planted trees will not need feeding until their second year following planting. This is because there are enough nutrients in the soil to keep them fit and healthy during early establishment. The tree's initial main aim is to produce anchor roots and find water.

During the second year, apply a general, well-balanced garden fertilizer – preferably an organic one. It should contain nitrogen, potassium and phosphorus and be spread across the mulched surface of the planting hole and then watered in.

Checking supports
If the tree has been staked (see page 26), it is important to check the ties attaching the tree to the stake. This should be done at various stages during the first year after planting. If they are tight and restricting the tree's growth, they will need to be loosened slightly, allowing the tree to grow and expand in stem diameter. Also check that the tree is not rubbing anywhere or being strangled on the tree stake. See also Tree-staking damage, page 139.

At the start of the second growing season, if the tree was planted correctly and given all the aftercare described above, it should be able to stand upright on its own without the need of a tree stake and ties. To check the tree's stability, undo the tree ties and, if the tree can support itself, the stake should be removed. Leaving a tree supported for too long makes it weaker as it relies too much on the support. Young trees need to be able to move in the wind as this prepares them for storms and bad weather as they mature.

TREE PROPAGATION
If you want to guarantee the ornamental attributes such as the flowering, leaf colour, bark effect and form of a tree, then you must grow it vegetatively, either from cuttings or grafting. Grafting is a more technical horticultural task requiring compatible rootstocks, clean scion material, sharp knives and skilled technique, so is best left to the expert nurseries. However, taking stem cuttings is much easier and can be done with secateurs, a sharp knife and limited facilities in the garden.

Sowing
By far the easiest and most successful method of propagating a tree is using seed – as the saying goes, 'Mighty oaks from little acorns grow.' This is true, and sowing can be done usually in autumn whenever the acorns are available. Don't be afraid to try growing your own trees from any seeds that you find on the ground in the garden or park. It can be very rewarding and it's free. Most trees grown in a nursery are usually produced from seeds, and we call this sexual propagation.

Some seeds have dormancy built into them as a means of holding back germination to the perfect time and to spread the germination period to avoid adverse weather conditions. This means that the seed may need a winter or two to break the dormancy down, so germination could take a year or two. Therefore, patience may be needed.

Before going to the trouble of sowing the seeds, first check their viability by sacrificing one or two, cutting each in half and seeing if there is a healthy, white, fertile embryo inside. Then follow the instructions in Growing a tree from seed, page 58.

Stem cuttings

There are three types of cuttings: hardwood, softwood and semi-ripe. **Hardwood cuttings** can be used for propagating trees such as willow (*Salix*), poplar (*Populus*), dogwood (*Cornus*), mulberry (*Morus*) and plane (*Platanus*) and should be done during the dormant season, that is, between mid-autumn and late winter.

Take healthy cuttings, 15–30cm/ 6–12in long, of about pencil thickness from vigorous shoots that have grown during the previous year. With a pair of sharp secateurs, make a horizontal cut immediately below a bud at the bottom of each cutting, and then a sloping cut just above a bud at the top. Dip the flat end of each cutting in a hormone rooting powder, to encourage root initiation and prevent it from rotting. Position cuttings 10–15cm/4–6in apart on well-cultivated soil in the ground or a cold frame for protection or into a container of free-draining compost, made up of 50:50 potting compost

This is a perfect hardwood cutting of a willow (*Salix*) with clean cuts at the top and bottom. It is ready to be inserted into free-draining compost.

such as John Innes No. 2 and coarse grit, in an unheated greenhouse. Then gently push about two-thirds of each cutting into the soil. Water in and leave alone, keeping the soil moist until the following autumn, by which time the cuttings will have rooted. Once this occurs, pot them up and grow on.

This perfect softwood cutting of an evergreen maple (*Acer* sp.) has had its soft tip and lower leaves removed with a sharp knife or secateurs. It is ready for insertion into cuttings compost.

Softwood cuttings are a good way of propagating trees such as birch (*Betula*), magnolia (*Magnolia*), lime (*Tilia*) and cherry (*Prunus*) in late spring or summer, when the young shoots are still soft.

Using a sharp knife, take a healthy cutting, 5–10cm/2–4in long, from just below a bud on the parent plant. Remove the lower leaves and pinch out the soft tip with a knife or fingers, then dip the base of the cutting into hormone rooting compound. Fill a pot with compost comprising 50:50 potting compost such as John Innes No. 2 and sharp sand, and insert the cuttings, 2.5–4cm/1–1½in apart, using a pencil or a dibber, with the leaves just above the level of the compost.

Water the cuttings in, cover the pot with a plastic bag to retain humidity, and place in good light and somewhere warm. Regularly ventilate the cuttings by temporarily lifting off the bag. Keep the compost moist until the cuttings are rooted, which can take several weeks. Once rooted, remove the bag and harden off the cuttings for two weeks. This involves gradually firming up the young plants by getting them used to the outdoor environment. Then pot them on, to help them develop strong root systems.

Semi-ripe cuttings are a suitable way of propagating evergreen trees and some conifers. The operation

ABOVE One of the easiest ways to propagate a yew tree (*Taxus baccata*) is to take semi-ripe cuttings during late summer.

BELOW About six months after taking the semi-ripe cutting, fresh, new, white roots will be growing from the base, ready for potting up.

is similar to softwood cuttings (see opposite) except that it is carried out in late summer, when the cutting is hard with a soft tip.

Remove some healthy shoots and trim each cutting to 10–15cm/4–6in long, slicing just below a leaf node; then remove the lowest leaves and the soft tip. Dip each cutting in hormone rooting powder and push it gently, 2.5–4cm/ 1–1½in deep, into a pot containing potting compost such as John Innes No. 2. Water well and cover with a plastic bag. Thereafter, treat as softwood cuttings. It may take until the following spring for the cuttings to have rooted sufficiently to pot on.

RESPONSIBILITIES OF TREE OWNERS

If you have a tree in your garden, you have a general duty of care not to cause injury to your neighbour, visitors and passers-by, and you may be negligent if the tree sheds a branch or fails, and injury or damage results. There is no golden rule as to how often a tree should be inspected, but if you failed to examine your tree and it caused damage or harm you would be negligent. It is therefore important to regularly check your trees for obvious defects and take appropriate action, especially after strong winds or adverse weather. If the trunk is covered in ivy, be sure to look underneath it, as ivy can hide a multitude of defects.

Seven obvious defects to look out for are:

- damaged, split or hanging branches;
- dead branches retaining their dead leaves in summer;
- a leaning tree with a recent change in orientation;
- exposed roots and recent root failure or movement;
- fungal fruiting bodies of decay fungi (see page 134);
- cankers and open decayed cavities;
- weak, V-shaped forks.

If you have any doubts or concerns as to the safety of your tree, it is recommended that you bring in a qualified competent arborist to carry out a professional inspection. Be sure to save the report as future evidence that the tree has been inspected, and make sure that the recommended mitigation works are carried out by the recommended date. See also When and how to hire a professional arborist, page 45.

PRUNING TREES

Why prune your tree, because not all trees need such treatment? Pruning is an art and a science brought together, and, before attempting to carry it out, it is important to understand the reason for pruning, and why you might want to do it now. This is key to the successful outcome of the pruning operation, as only by knowing what it is you would like to achieve as the final outcome can you determine how you will prune the tree and which branches will be removed.

First of all, before doing any tree work, it is important to check that the tree is yours to prune and not your neighbour's, especially if it is growing on a boundary. Even if it is yours, it's best to seek permission from the neighbour first and avoid any unnecessary disputes.

Never attempt to prune a large mature tree with a trunk that has a diameter over 7cm/3in measured at 1.5m/5ft above ground level without first checking whether there are any legal restrictions that apply, such as the tree being protected by law by a Tree Preservation Order (TPO) or that it grows in a Conservation Area. This can be discovered by calling the planning department of your local council. Failure to do this and carrying out any tree work without the planning permission of the local planning authority will break the law. If permission is appropriate, an application will need to be completed and submitted to the relevant planning department.

Understanding the biology of tree pruning

On the top of every branch is a branch bark ridge (which resembles a Fu Manchu moustache) and at the branch attachment lies a branch collar (a swollen part on the underside of the branch). These two areas of the tree should never be compromised by cutting into them, as they produce a reaction zone underneath the bark within this area that can compartmentalize wounds, heal them and prevent invasion from fungal decay.

Therefore, to do the final cut in the three-cut method (see page 40), position the saw blade against the branch collar on the branch-side of the tree and line up the cut to avoid cutting into the collar. This should leave a circular pruning wound with no jagged edges, which will eventually heal over from the outside inwards like a doughnut. This final pruning cut is known as 'natural target pruning'. If it is made correctly, the tree will be able to repair and protect the wound without any further intervention.

Branch bark ridge

Branch collar

So why do we prune trees?
Some of the many reasons for pruning
include:

- remove the 3Ds – dead, diseased
  and dying branches;
- produce a clean stem or trunk free
  of any lateral branches and allow
  improved access under the tree for
  pedestrians or vehicles;
- help the tree to form a well-balanced
  crown by removing over-extended
  branches;
- reduce the end weight of branches or
  alter or reduce the overall shape of
  the crown;
- allow more light to a property or
  garden through a dense leafy canopy;
- encourage flowers and fruit for
  ornamental or edible purposes;
- for health and safety, such as by
  removing dangerous branches that
  may cause injury to people or
  damage to property.

Understanding what to prune
There are several principles that, if
followed, will help the pruner gain
a clear knowledge of what to prune.
These are known as the SHARP
principles and they are easy to
remember because that's what your
pruning tools should be.

S – is for the tree **species**. Knowing the
species of tree that you are pruning will
inform the pruner of how it naturally
grows and how it will respond to the
secateurs and saw;
H – understand the growth **habit** and
form of the tree (see page 13);
A – what are the ornamental **attributes**
that you are growing this tree for –
flowers, ornamental or edible fruit,
leaves (shape, size, colour) or bark?
R – what are the **reasons** for pruning?
P – is for the **principles** of pruning
and how the tree will be pruned to
successfully achieve the required
outcome.

Pruning kit
Before attempting to carry out any
pruning operation, it is – like planting
– important to have the right tools for
the job. The perfect pruning kit will
include:

- a pruning saw with a scabbard;
- a pair of good-quality secateurs,
  preferably bypass ones. These work
  like a pair of sharp scissors by
  cutting the branch rather than
  crushing the stem, which anvil-type
  secateurs are more likely to do;
- a holster to carry the secateurs in;
- a pair of good-quality thornproof
  gloves;
- eye protection;
- a small wetstone or a purpose-made
  diamond sharpening tool
- white spirit or a silicone cleaner;
- a first-aid kit.

The scabbard and holster will help to
keep the tools clean and protect their
cutting parts from being damaged or
accidentally cutting the pruner. There
are several makes of both pruning
saws and secateurs available in garden
centres and online, and my advice
is to buy the best quality that you
can afford. A good set will last you
a lifetime if each tool is looked after,
by cleaning and sharpening regularly

The ideal all-round pruning kit for most tree pruning jobs in the garden includes: secateurs with a holster and sharpening stone; a pruning saw and scabbard; and a silicone cleaner.

(see Maintenance of equipment, below). Because modern pruning tools are extremely sharp, it is important to wear a pair of protective gloves, especially on the hand not using the saw or secateurs. Some trees have sharp spines or thorns, so eye protection is advisable in this instance.

Maintenance of equipment
Cleaning tools during and after use is important to ensure a smooth operating action and to remove any build-up of sap, gum and conifer resins. This can be done each day with white spirit or a silicone cleaner, followed by a wipe down using an oily cloth to prevent any rust.

An important part of biosecurity is to sterilize pruning tools with a disinfectant or household bleach between trees that may be infected with a disease, in order to help minimize disease transmission. If bleach is used, it should be mixed at a ratio of 10 per cent bleach to 90 per cent water; dip the tool in the solution, and then wipe it over with an oily rag, as bleach is corrosive and otherwise will cause long-term damage to your tool.

A pair of good-quality bypass secateurs can be adjusted easily and should be resharpened regularly before the cutting blades become

Keep your secateurs sharp by regularly honing the edge of the blade. Pruning will then be easy to carry out, and you will reduce the possibility of tearing the branch.

too blunt. This can be done with a small wetstone or a purpose-made diamond sharpening tool. Modern pruning saws cannot be sharpened and once the cutting blade is dull a replacement blade should be fitted.

When is the best time to prune trees? The general rule is to prune when the tree's energy levels are at their highest, so that the tree has the ability to repair any pruning wounds without stressing itself. This will be during the dormant season in winter, when the tree has shed all its leaves, or else during the height of summer when the tree is in full leaf and busy producing sugars

and starch. However, damaged or dangerous branches should be removed when seen at any time of the year.

Some trees, if pruned at the wrong time of the year, will bleed from the cuts, so these should be tackled when they have produced all their new leaves or when they are fully dormant in mid-winter. Such tree genera include walnuts (*Juglans*), hickories (*Carya*), maples (*Acer*) and birches (*Betula*). Some fruit trees and rosaceous species are prone to a fungal disease called silver leaf, so they should be pruned in summer, when the disease is not around to infect the tree through the old pruning cuts.

The cutting blade on the secateurs should always be against the branch that remains on the tree to ensure a clean final cut at the correct distance from the parent branch.

Caution: Watch out for nesting birds and avoid nesting season, especially when cutting hedges.

How to prune trees

It is best to remove unwanted branches as soon as possible in their life to avoid large pruning wounds. This is best done by rubbing off unwanted buds and young shoots with the thumb, preventing them from turning woody. However, the next best thing is to remove small branches that are of pencil thickness (less than 1cm/½in) with a pair of sharp secateurs rather than leaving them and then needing to use a saw later. Always prune each back to a strong-growing lateral

Pruning safety tips

Do use:
- sharp clean pruning tools and regularly resharpen them;
- hand and eye protection, and have a first-aid kit to hand.

Do not use:
- a carpenter's saw for pruning trees; always use a pruning saw;
- a ladder on your own;
- tree paints.

In the three-cut method for removing a branch, (top left) first undercut the branch, then (top right) saw the top cut about one-third of the branch diameter away from the first cut.

When done correctly (above left), a step cut will have been made. For the final cut (above right), place the side of the saw blade against the branch bark ridge beyond the collar.

branch or cut back to the parent branch or trunk. A protruding stump should never be left, as it will look unsightly and the pruning wound may not heal and will eventually die back, causing decay.

To remove a larger branch, it is important first to reduce most of the weight, to avoid it tearing back into the trunk of the tree or parent branch, which will likely cause damage to the tree; then the final cut is made. This technique is known as the 'three-cut method'. To prune in this way, from the branch attachment on the tree trunk work back along the branch to a suitable position for the undercut; then, with the saw, create an undercut of about one-third

of the diameter of the branch. Stop cutting before the weight of the branch pinches the saw. Then, at a distance of about one-third of the diameter of the branch away from the undercut, make a top cut. Never try to line the cuts up. When the top cut levels up with the undercut the branch will snap off cleanly, without tearing back. The final pruning cut can now be made back to the trunk or parent branch (see page 35).

Tree paints and wound dressings
Providing you follow the principles of natural target pruning (see page 35), there is no need to use tree paints to cover up wounds. If anything, tree

After coppicing hazel (*Corylus avellana*) there will be plenty of regrowth after one or two years, providing a fresh new plant.

paints can hinder repair because many were bitumen-based and created a microclimate underneath, so were a perfect breeding ground for micro-organisms. *Don't paint tree wounds.*

MATURE TREE PRUNING OPERATIONS

There are several pruning operations that are carried out on trees, whether they are young, mature, small or large, but the principles are the same for all. As a rough guide, you should avoid removing more live branches than is necessary – and certainly no more than 25 per cent of the tree's foliage or buds in a growing season.

Coppicing or stooling
In late winter or early spring, a single-trunked tree is pruned to around 7cm/3in from ground level to create a multi-stemmed tree or large shrub. This can be done on a regular cycle to rejuvenate trees that tolerate hard pruning, like beech (*Fagus*), yew (*Taxus*), lime (*Tilia*), hazel (*Corylus*), willow (*Salix*) and mulberry (*Morus*). Coppicing can also be carried out to create larger leaves on trees like foxglove tree (*Paulownia*) and *Catalpa* and to highlight coloured stems on dogwoods (*Cornus*) and willows (*Salix*). See also Creating a multi-stemmed birch, page 66.

Well-pleached large-leaved limes (*Tilia platyphyllos*) can provide a very architectural feature in the garden during winter and summer.

Crown lifting

In this technique, the lower branches are pruned off to increase the space between the ground and lowest branches. This improves access under the canopy and allows more light through to a border or lawn under the lower branches.

Crown reduction

In crown reduction, pruning is done to make a tree smaller by height or width while still maintaining as natural a shape as possible. Any branches that are shortened should be cut back to a strong lateral branch and not to a stub end.

Crown thinning

Lateral branches are pruned to thin the canopy and reduce the overall density of the leaf cover, allowing more daylight and wind to penetrate the crown. When this operation is carried out, the branches should be thinned evenly throughout the crown. No more than 25 per cent of leaf should be removed in one growing season.

Formative pruning

This is done on young trees, getting them off to a good start towards maturity by encouraging a strong, well-branched crown with a little help. Formative pruning includes removing: the '3Ds'

When done on an annual cycle, pollarding can be used on some species to maintain a smaller tree in a restricted space or to generate masses of coloured stems from the pruning knuckles.

large-leaved lime (*Tilia platyphyllos*), hornbeam (*Carpinus betulus*), field maple (*Acer campestre*), fruiting apples (*Malus domestica* cultivars) and holm oak (*Quercus ilex*). As with pollarding and coppicing, pleached hedges need to be pruned on an annual cycle to maintain them during the early stages of growth as well as once they are established.

Pollarding
This form of ornamental crown reduction should be started when the tree is still young and soon after it is established. The pruning operation is done on an annual cycle, and growths are pruned back to a knuckle, which will form following regular pruning in the same place.

Selective pruning
Individual live branches are removed or shortened in order to maintain a symmetrical crown shape (such as a standard topiary ball, see page 110) or else if a single branch is extending out of the canopy and interfering with a structure or another tree.

Suckers and water shoots
Young adventitious shoots that are generated from dormant buds in the tree's bark are known as suckers or water shoots. Suckers usually develop at the base of a tree, while water shoots grow on the main trunk or branches. Unless they are needed as a form of coppicing (see page 41) or pleaching (see left), suckers and water shoots should be removed as close to the tree as soon as possible, using secateurs or a pruning saw.

(see So why do we prune trees?, page 36); any twin leaders that are likely to produce a weak crown later in life; crossing branches; extended branches that will cause an unbalanced crown; and lower branches in order to expose the trunk.

Pleaching
This is a method of pruning and training trees, sometimes known as 'espaliers', to produce a narrow hedge on trunks. Young shoots are trained and woven together on a temporary framework to the desired shape and form as a high screen above a low fence or wall and can be further trained to form arches, arbours and tunnels. Trees that pleach well include

Some grafted ornamental or fruit trees may produce suckers from the rootstock below the graft union. If not removed, they will grow faster than the grafted scion and take over the specimen tree, so deal with them as soon as they appear. If they are soft and fleshy, they can be rubbed off the trunk with the thumb.

DISPOSAL OF ARISINGS

Before any work is carried out on a tree, especially when hiring an arborist, both parties should agree what will be done with the arisings (prunings). Most arborists will have some form of mechanical chipper that will convert the branches into woodchip, which can be used as a mulch in garden borders or around trees, or else be composted or taken away. Wood stacks can also be made as 'ecological piles' as a means of creating a habitat for wildlife and fungi in the wilder parts of a garden (see Building an ecological log stack, page 70).

Do not burn arisings from pruning unless there is no alternative.

Tree stump removal

Stumps can be retained alive or dead in the garden and should be cut as low to the ground as possible to prevent a trip hazard. If retained alive, they can be allowed to sprout new shoots and regenerate as a coppice (see page 41). Alternatively, if a retained stump is not desired, it can be dug out by hand or machine, although this can be quite a physically demanding task; easier still, it can be ground out with a mechanical stump grinder.

A very efficient way to remove a tree stump following the felling of a tree is to grind it out with a stump grinder, which should be operated by a professional contractor.

TREE REMOVAL

Small young trees can be cut down without too much of a problem, but for larger specimens this may be the time to bring in a professional arborist who has the knowledge, experience and insurance to carry out this scale of work. Due to restricted space in most domestic gardens, trees will need to be dismantled in sections rather than being felled in one piece, to avoid potential damage to property or other trees in the garden.

Do not attempt to remove a large tree without professional expertise and only tackle a small tree with the appropriate tools and equipment (see Pruning kit, page 36).

Trained experienced arborists are skilled workers used to working at heights, with climbing ropes, specialist equipment and chainsaws. Never try such work yourself; always call in the arborist.

When and how to hire a professional arborist

There are many pruning operations that will need an experienced professional arborist to carry them out correctly and safely. Fully trained arborists know what they are doing and are very able to provide clear advice and guidance for any pruning operations that may be needed. They are used to working safely at heights and have all the appropriate safety equipment and tools to carry out the necessary tree works, and they are fully insured. To find one, contact professional societies such as the Arboricultural Association in the UK (www.trees.org.uk) or the International Society of Arboriculture in the USA (www.isa-arbor.com) for a list of approved arborists in your area.

Never use cold callers or anyone that knocks on your door offering to prune your tree. They are usually unskilled, uninsured, and will often prune only what they can reach from ladders. They may also leave the tree in an unsightly condition – generally needing further tree work to renovate it later in its life – or even kill it, and still charge high rates.

Plants

—

Silver wattle

Acacia dealbata aka mimosa

The silver wattle is a short-lived, vigorous, small evergreen tree from south-eastern Australia, with a trunk covered in a smooth blue bark with bipinnate, silvery, fern-like leaves. It produces masses of fragrant, bright yellow, globular flowers from late winter through to early spring, brightening up any dull overcast day.

Family Fabaceae	
Height 8–12m/26–40ft	
Spread 2.5–4m/8–13ft	
Habit Spreading	
Hardiness Zone 3: –5 to 1°C/23 to 33°F	
Position Full sun	

WHERE TO GROW

This tree needs some shelter or protection from cold strong winds, or else the foliage and canopy will be damaged as the branches are quite brittle. It grows well on free-draining, acid to neutral, sandy loams. Silver wattle is often planted in a small garden without enough space to develop and then requires hard pruning to make it fit, so give it plenty of room.

HOW TO GROW

This tree does not like being transplanted, so it is important to plant small, container-grown specimens and be patient. However, you will not have to wait long to see it flower (see also Planting a tree in a pot for a balcony, page 88).

TALCUM POWDER
In moist mountainous areas in Australia, a white lichen can cover the bark of silver wattle, giving it a silvery appearance and its species name *dealbata*, meaning 'covered in a white powder'.

GROWING TIP

As silver wattle is a vigorous grower, the top can outgrow the root system and the tree becomes unstable and needs post-planting staking to stay upright. To avoid this, prune early and hard to encourage a multi-stemmed tree with a stronger root system (see Creating a multi-stemmed birch, page 66).

Paperbark maple

Acer griseum

The main beauty of this tree is its paper-like, cinnamon-coloured, peeling bark, which provides year-round interest. Also on this tree are small trifoliate leaves, which turn a lovely orange-red in autumn, giving a little shade in the garden (see also Making a collage of autumnal leaves in a picture frame, page 50).

—

WHERE TO GROW

This is a beautiful small tree that will make a perfect solitary ornamental specimen in any garden with restricted space. It prefers a neutral to acid, moist but well-drained soil.

HOW TO GROW

This species is best planted as a small container-grown tree, as it is a slow grower and dislikes any root disturbance (see also Planting a tree in a pot for a balcony, page 88). It can be found in the nurseries as a small standard, feathered standard or multi-stemmed specimen.

GROWING TIP

Because most paperbark maples are grown from seed in the nursery, the texture and colour of the bark can vary considerably from tree to tree, so look for a good form with interesting and highly colourful bark. For another maple with interesting bark see Five hardworking trees for any small garden, page 78.

Family Sapindaceae

Height 10m/33ft

Spread 6m/20ft

Habit Rounded

Hardiness Zone 5: −15 to −10°C/5 to 14°F

Position Full sun or partial shade

Acer negundo 'Variegatum'

CHINA – THE MOTHER OF GARDENS
Paperbark maple is just one of the many trees introduced to our gardens from China by Ernest Henry Wilson in 1901.

Acer negundo

Making a collage of autumnal leaves in a picture frame

During autumn, gardens and parks come to life with all the vibrant reds, purples and yellows of the seasonal leaf colour. Such colouring is caused by trees stopping production of chlorophyl, which is the green pigment used in photosynthesis to absorb energy from sunlight. As this pigment disappears from the leaf, the other weaker pigments, which are produced in late summer and are obscured by the chlorophyl, are able to shine through and show off their true colours. These are the carotins, which are yellow and orange tones, and the anthocyanins, which are the reds and purples. For good autumn colour there needs to be some ground moisture, warm sunny days and cooler nights without frost.

This is a project for the autumn and serves as reminder of this season throughout the year. It's easy to do and makes a walk in the park or garden more exciting and interesting. All you require is a bag to collect the leaves in, to stop them drying out too quickly, a pile of old newspapers and a few large books to act as weights. To complete the project, you'll need a picture frame large enough to show off your leaves.

Preferably wait for a dry day and collect a variety of leaves, with a mixture of colours, sizes and shapes. When you get home, spread out the leaves between sheets of newspaper and place a few heavy books on top of the pile of filled newspapers. Bring the pile indoors, and place, preferably, in warm and dry spot. Leave for a few days to dry while pressed; it may be necessary to change the newspapers occasionally, especially if the leaves are slightly damp.

After they have dried, lay out the leaves in a pattern of your choice and offer up to the picture frame. Once you are happy with the design and layout, seal the frame and hang it on the wall.

1. Collect various autumn leaves in the garden.
2. Lay the leaves out on the newspaper and cover with more sheets of newspaper.
3. Place heavy books on top of the newspapers to press the leaves and stop them shrivelling up. Leave to dry for a few days.
4. Arrange the leaves in the picture frame in an artistic way. Then seal its back.
5. Hang the final picture on the wall at home.

Japanese maple

Acer palmatum

There are so many cultivars on offer, with many leaf shapes and colours throughout the year, that it will be difficult to select one for your garden. But, in the end, choice will come down to personal preference and availability of plants in the nursery. The foliage is also useful in craft projects (see Making a collage of autumnal leaves in a picture frame, page 50).

Family	Sapindaceae
Height	2.5–4m/8–13ft
Spread	2.5–4m/8–13ft
Habit	Vase, columnar, spreading or weeping
Hardiness	Zone 5: –15 to –10°C/5 to 14°F
Position	Partial shade

WHERE TO GROW

These maples prefer a fertile, moist but well-drained soil and, because of the nature of their growth and size, are perfect for the small garden or as a specimen on a rock garden or in a border. They also make good container plants for the patio or balcony (see also Planting a tree in a pot for a balcony, page 88).

HOW TO GROW

Make sure you buy your tree from the nursery as small container-grown stock and enjoy watching it grow, rather than planting a larger specimen which will likely take considerably more time to become accustomed to its new home.

GROWING TIP

All Japanese maple cultivars are grown for their special attributes and are grafted on to a rootstock, so be sure not to plant them too deep, thereby covering up the graft union. See also Suckers and water shoots, page 43.

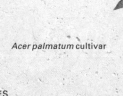

Acer palmatum cultivar

Acer palmatum cultivar

NOTABLE CULTIVARS AND ANOTHER NOTABLE SPECIES

- 'Bloodgood' is a large shrubby tree to 10m/33ft, with blood-red, palmate leaves.
- 'Burgundy Lace' is a small graceful tree to 3m/10ft, with finely cut, light red-purple leaves.
- 'Dissectum' makes a low, broad, spreading tree to 4m/13ft, with mid-green, dissected leaves that turn orange to bright red in autumn.
- 'Enkan' has a rounded habit to 3m/10ft if trained, with five lobed, deeply divided, palmate, bronze to maroon leaves that turn bright red in autumn.
- 'Orange Dream' is a vase-shaped maple growing to 3m/10ft, with golden yellow leaves with pink edges.
- 'Osakazuki' is a small tree, to 4m/13ft, with the reputedly best autumn colour of all the Japanese maples.
- *A. japonicum* makes a small, multi-stemmed tree to 8m/26ft, with outstanding autumn colour. There is also a delightful cultivar called 'Aconitifolium' with deeply dissected leaves.

WHEN EAST MEETS WEST
All of the Japanese maples add a touch of Japan and colour to any garden.

Norway maple
Acer platanoides

The species name *platanoides* means 'like a plane tree' because the leaves are very similar except that they are arranged oppositely on the twigs. Norway maple is a popular shade tree from northern Europe with greenish yellow flowers that appear before the leaves in spring. Its golden/orange autumn leaf colour is as good as on any other maple (see also Making a collage of autumnal leaves in a picture frame, page 50).

Family	Sapindaceae
Height	15–25m/50–82ft
Spread	10–20m/33–66ft
Habit	Rounded
Hardiness	Zone 7: <–20°C/–4°F
Position	Full sun

WHERE TO GROW
This maple is tough and will grow in any soil type that is moist and free-draining, but it seeds readily and this can be a problem so you may prefer to plant a cultivar instead.

HOW TO GROW
There are many cultivars available in tree nurseries and garden centres, some of which have better leaf colours, shapes and forms than the species.

GROWING TIP
If you plant the variegated cultivar 'Drummondii', you will need to keep an eye out for reversion, which is when the leaves turn from variegated back to plain green. Prune out any reverted branch as soon as possible, to retain the variegation.

A VIOLIN CONCERTO
It is believed that the famed Stradivarius violins may have used Norway maple in their construction.

NOTABLE CULTIVARS

- 'Crimson King' has striking dark red foliage and a rounded crown shape.
- 'Drummondii' is a slower grower; it has lime-green leaves with creamy white margins.
- 'Globosum' retains a rounded, almost spherical shape and can be grown as a standard on a trunk (see Creating a standard topiary ball, page 110) or as a ball without a trunk.
- 'Royal Red' has striking dark red foliage and a rounded crown shape.

Indian horse chestnut

Aesculus indica aka Indian buckeye

There are approximately twenty species of *Aesculus*, which all make good ornamental garden trees, and there is a size – large or small – for any garden; they should not be confused with the sweet chestnut (*Castanea sativa*). The Indian horse chestnut is becoming a widely planted tree due to its resistance to the horse chestnut leaf miner (see page 132), because the toxins in its leaves render them poisonous to the larvae of the leaf miner. The leaves emerge a pinky bronze colour and quickly turn green with little or no autumn colour. Indian horse chestnut is free-flowering with large upright candles of cream flowers spotted yellow then red, which are perfect for summer-pollinating insects, especially bees.

Family Sapindaceae	
Height 15m/50ft	
Spread 15m/50ft	
Habit Rounded	
Hardiness Zone 5: −15 to −10°C/5 to 14°F	
Position Full sun	

WHERE TO GROW

The Indian horse chestnut makes a tree very similar in habit to the European horse chestnut (*Aesculus hippocastanum*), but flowers later in the season, from late spring to early summer. It is a large tree with a spreading crown, so needs a garden with plenty of space to grow to its best potential. Plant in any moist but well-drained soil.

HOW TO GROW

This tree can be planted in a variety of sizes from a one-year-old whip to an extra-heavy standard. To be sure of quick and successful establishment, the best size will be a small standard with a good root ball or a tree that has been container-grown in the nursery.

GROWING TIP

Most of the horse chestnuts or buckeyes are easily germinated from a conker, so why not try growing your own? See Growing a tree from a seed, page 58.

Aesculus parviflora

THE EYE OF A DEER
In North America, the common name for a tree in the genus *Aesculus* is 'buckeye' as the shiny seed resembles the eye of a deer. In Europe they are called 'horse chestnuts' because of the horseshoe-shaped leaf scars on the twigs.

NOTABLE CULTIVAR AND OTHER NOTABLE SPECIES

- 'Sydney Pearce' is a cultivar of *A. indica* raised at Kew Gardens in 1932, which has a more rounded crown and is more floriferous than the species.
- *A. californica* is a large shrub or small tree to 12m/40ft, with an unruly canopy bearing upright cream flower panicles, up to 30cm/12in tall, which can last for up to six weeks.
- *A. glabra* (Ohio buckeye) makes a tree to 25m/82ft tall, with a rounded crown and pale yellow to yellow-green flowers.
- *A. hippocastanum* (horse chestnut) is a magnificent tree but suffers badly from the horse chestnut leaf miner.
- *A. parviflora* (bottlebrush buckeye) is a small suckering tree or shrub to 5m/16ft, with cream flower panicles in summer.
- *A. pavia* (red buckeye) is a large shrub or small tree to 8m/26ft, with dark red flowers in spring.

Growing a tree from a seed

When you go out for a walk in the park, it's always very rewarding to collect a seed or two, sow it, grow it and plant it in the garden, and it's easy – anyone can do it.

First of all, collect the seed. One of the most recognizable is the conker of the horse chestnut (*Aesculus hippocastanum*) or an acorn from an oak (*Quercus*). It's best to sow seeds as soon as possible after collecting them, but if you can't you can store them in the refrigerator for a short period of time. Remove each seed (conker in this project) from its spiny shell and find a pot large enough to take it, but not so large that it will be lost in the pot or rot off because the compost gets too wet.
For this project I used a pot of 30cm/12in diameter.

Place some crocks in the bottom of the pot for good drainage (see Planting a tree in a pot for a balcony, page 88) and top up to just below the rim with seed compost. This is light and open for seeds to easily root into, and has no fertilizer, which can be too rich for young seedlings.

Gently push the conker into the compost with just the top of the conker showing on the surface. Then sprinkle the surface with compost to prevent moss and algae growing and to stop water splash. Label the pot, then water the conker into the compost, and place the pot in an open cold frame or somewhere else safe in the garden, open to the elements. You may need to cover the pot with fine wire netting to protect it from birds or rodents, which may take a fancy to the conker during the colder months of the year.

During early spring the conker will germinate, producing a root to anchor it into the compost and a shoot with fresh leaves.

Its pot will be large enough for the young tree until the following autumn, when it will need to be repotted in good-quality, soil-based potting compost, such as John Innes No. 3 compost, or be planted in the garden. Be sure to give the young plant plenty of water through the year and do not allow the soil to dry out.

1. Fill the pot with a seed compost.
2. Push the conker into the surface of the compost with the top of the conker just showing.
3. Cover the surface with a dusting of compost.
4. Label the pot to indicate what seed was sown and when it was planted.
5. Finish the job by watering well. Then set the pot in a cold frame or open garden.
6. Less than twelve months later, the young tree is ready for growing on or planting in the garden.

Grey alder

Alnus incana

The grey alder is a small to medium-sized tree with smooth grey bark, shallow roots and small, dark green leaves. The male flowers are yellow-brown, pendulous catkins appearing in late winter or early spring before the leaves, and they are wind-pollinated. The female catkins turn into oval, woody, cone-like fruits in autumn, bearing small winged seeds. These are released as the cone opens and are dispersed by the wind.

—

WHERE TO GROW

The alders are closely associated with water and will grow in most soil types including poorly or well-drained, low-fertile soils and will stand a range of pH from acid to alkaline. They will tolerate anaerobic conditions, wet or dry. Some of the ornamental cultivars deserve a position in the garden and make good screen and shelter-belt trees as they are resistant to windy conditions.

HOW TO GROW

Alder are fast-growing and if planted as small feathered trees will soon establish, and the trunks can be cleaned up to the desired height of clear stem. They also make good standard trees if grown as specimens in a border or lawn.

GROWING TIP

Because alders are fast-growing, keep an eye on the fleshy leader; it may be necessary to support the trunk with a bamboo cane to develop and maintain its straightness.

Family Betulaceae	
Height 12–17m/40–56ft	
Spread 5m/16ft	
Habit Columnar	
Hardiness Zone 7: <−20°C/−4°F	
Position Full sun	

NOTABLE CULTIVAR AND OTHER NOTABLE SPECIES

- 'Aurea' bears young shoots and leaves that emerge a golden yellow, as well as red catkins that open a pinky yellow.
- *A. cordata* (Italian alder) is an elegant, fast-growing tree to 25m/82ft.
- *A. glutinosa* (common alder) has a conical habit and delightful yellow catkins in spring. 'Imperialis' is an elegant, slow-growing alder with deeply cut, fern-like leaves.
- *A. rubra* (red alder) is the largest of the alders, reaching 20–30m/66–100ft, and is a native of the west coast of North America.

WATER CARR
As well as thriving by water, the alder's second-preferred habitat is boggy ground, which develops into pure alder woodland, known as a carr.

Serviceberry

Amelanchier canadensis aka mespilus, shadbush

All the *Amelanchier* species probably have more common names than any other tree. They are small deciduous trees grown in the garden for their showy white flowers. These can appear at the same time as the new, bronze-coloured leaves, which then serve as a background for the flowers.

—

WHERE TO GROW

Serviceberries will fit any situation in the garden, whether it be a formal or an informal setting. They are low-maintenance when grown in a moist but well-drained, lime-free soil. To get the best out of them in autumn, ensure that they are planted in a sunny position.

HOW TO GROW

Let serviceberries grow naturally, and do not try to train them into a formal standard tree as they are shrubby with a spreading habit. Some species and cultivars do have upright-growing branches and can be trained as a standard, but most will be multi-stemmed in the nursery. *Amelanchier canadensis* is suckering with upright stems.

GROWING TIP

If you are growing these trees in a garden in a rural setting you will need to protect them against deer and rabbits, which are partial to the foliage of these beautiful plants.

Q. When is a Mespilus not a medlar?
A. When it is an *Amelanchier* and a snowy mespilus. (All other medlars are in the genus *Mespilus*.)

Family Rosaceae

Height 4–8m/13–26ft

Spread 2.5–4m/8–13ft

Habit Spreading

Hardiness Zone 7: <–20°C/–4°F

Position Full sun or partial shade

OTHER NOTABLE SPECIES AND CULTIVARS

- *A. alnifolia* 'Obelisk' (alder-leaved serviceberry) has a columnar form and a good show of flowers as well as superb autumn colour.
- *A.* × *grandiflora* 'Ballerina' is a small tree with an abundance of small white flowers in spring and with red autumn colour.
- *A.* × *grandiflora* 'Robin Hill' is a small tree with dense upright branches and pink flowers that turn to pure white as they mature.
- *A.* × *lamarckii* is a small shrubby tree with beautiful white flowers in spring and copper-coloured new leaves, which turn green as they mature.

Strawberry tree

Arbutus unedo

This is perfect for planting in the garden as an evergreen screen tree with tough, dark green, leathery leaves. It also has decorative, brown, shedding bark on the trunk and main branches as well as white to light pink, pendent, bell-shaped flowers followed by strawberry-like fruits – hence the common name. However, it is not related to the common strawberry.

—

WHERE TO GROW

As this tree is a member of the Ericaceae family it prefers a neutral to acid, well-drained soil, but will grow in lightly alkaline soils. It will also tolerate some salt-laden winds, so is a good tree for exposed sites near the seaside.

HOW TO GROW

Buy strawberry tree as a container-grown plant, as like most ericaceous trees it has shallow fibrous roots and does not like disturbance. After planting in the garden, be sure to give it plenty of mulch around the root plate to stop the shallow roots drying out.

GROWING TIP

During the first three to five years after planting, give some protection from cold winds, but once established strawberry tree is very hardy and will tolerate some dry conditions. If it becomes unruly with an unbalanced crown, cut it back quite hard to shape in late spring before it starts to grow so it can fill in the gaps caused by the pruning.

Family Ericaceae	
Height 5–10m/16–33ft	
Spread 10m/33ft	
Habit Rounded	
Hardiness Zone 5: –15 to –10°C/5 to 14°F	
Position Full sun or partial shade	

OTHER NOTABLE SPECIES AND HYBRIDS

- *A. andrachne* (Grecian strawberry tree) has a smooth peeling bark revealing a layer of green bark, gradually changing to a bright orange-brown.
- *A. × andrachnoides* is a hybrid between *A. unedo* and *A. andrachne*, with cinnamon-brown bark on older trees.
- *A. menziesii* (Pacific madrone, madroño) is a difficult tree to grow in cultivation, but if you are successful it has the best multi-coloured, peeling bark of any tree and is certainly worth trying in your garden.

ONCE EATEN, TWICE SHY
Pliny the Elder is reputed to have said '*unum tantum edo*', which means 'I eat only one' because of the bland taste of the fruit. Thus the species name is *unedo*.

Silver birch

Betula pendula

The silver birch is a very elegant, medium-sized tree with silvery peeling bark on mature trunks and slender pendent twigs, resembling a weeping tree, hence the species name. The green leaves are small and diamond-shaped and turn butter-yellow in autumn.

—

WHERE TO GROW

This is a pioneer species and is not fussy about where it grows, tolerating any soil types providing they are moist but free-draining. There is a place in every garden for a birch, as a solitary specimen or in a group showing off the special bark effect on the trunks.

HOW TO GROW

When planted in areas with little air pollution, the white-barked birches sometimes lose their whiteness to algal growth on the trunks. Use a soft sponge soaked in a bucket of warm water containing a dash of washing-up liquid to help maintain those white silhouettes through the winter months.

GROWING TIP

Birches are grown mainly for their attractive bark, but they can look so much better in the garden if they have multiple stems or trunks to show off more of that special attribute. See Creating a multi-stemmed birch, page 66.

Family Betulaceae	
Height 12m/40ft	
Spread 6m/20ft	
Habit Oval or weeping	
Hardiness Zone 7: <−20°C/−4°F	
Position Full sun or partial shade	

OTHER NOTABLE SPECIES AND CULTIVARS

There are many highly ornamental cultivars of birches available in the nurseries and garden centres, and personal preference will be the deciding factor on which to plant. Below are just a select few.

- *B. ermanii* (Erman's birch) is native to Japan and the Russian Far East and is a hardy birch with yellow, finely peeling bark; it's the first to drop its leaves in autumn. 'Grayswood Hill' is a lovely cultivar with peeling, creamy white bark and pronounced lenticels (the pores in the bark that the tree breathes through), which can be ornamental.
- *B. nigra* (river birch) is from North America and produces very attractive, orange, flaky bark; it will grow in most conditions including wet and dry. Heritage (aka 'Cully') is a popular clonal selection.
- *B. papyrifera* (paper birch) displays virgin white, peeling bark as the tree matures.
- *B. pendula* 'Youngii' (Young's weeping birch) makes a low domed tree and is often top-worked (grafted on to the top of a short trunk).
- *B. pubescens* (downy birch) is a British native, like *B. pendula*, but has has more upright twigs and hairy stems.
- *B. utilis* subsp. *albosinensis* (red-bark birch, Chinese red birch), from the mountains of western China, displays different colours of finely peeling bark from red to orange, depending on the cultivar. 'Red Panda' and 'Fascination' are two popular cultivars worthy of a place in the garden.
- *B. utilis* subsp. *jacquemontii* (Himalayan birch) bears the brightest white bark of any birch. 'Doorenbos' is a beautiful tree with upright branches and striking white bark. 'Grayswood Ghost' is one of the best forms of white-barked birches.

WHERE ARE WE?
In North America, the indigenous people used the bark of the paper birch for canoes, wigwams, scrolls and maps, including the oldest maps of North America.

Betula nigra Heritage (aka 'Cully')

Creating a multi-stemmed birch

One of the many attributes of birches (*Betula*) is their beautiful ornamental bark colour. To show this off to the best potential, several main trunks are better than one, and for that reason many nurseries grow and sell multi-stemmed specimens. Some tree nurseries plant three young trees together and allow them to develop into a multi-stemmed tree, but these can lead to structural problems later in life as they grow together.

The best way to produce a multi-stemmed birch is to prune a young plant low down on the trunk at ground level and allow it to produce suckers and train these to the number of stems required. Choose a good species or cultivar of your favourite birch; for suggestions see Silver birch, page 64. Grow your tree in a container for one year to develop a strong root system and a good stem, which should be about pencil thickness. Then, between autumn and spring, during the dormant season, cut back the main trunk to ground level with a pair of good-quality, sharp secateurs or a saw.

In spring the young tree will start to produce new suckering growth from the pruning wound, and the size of the root system will determine the vigour of this new young growth. As the new growths develop, they can be thinned out if there are too many stems, to leave the number required. Generally, three stems make a well-balanced specimen. You will soon have the making of a small, multi-stemmed birch ready to plant in the garden.

1 Choose a strong, healthy young birch tree (here, paper birch/*Betula papyrifera*).
2 Plant it in a large pot using a good-quality, soil-based potting compost.
3 Cover the compost surface with a clean mulch such as chipped bark.
4 Prune the stem 2.5cm/1in above the base of the trunk.
5 Fresh new shoots, generated from the pruning cut, will develop into a multi-stemmed birch tree showing off its attractive white bark.

Hornbeam

Carpinus betulus

The most popular hornbeam makes a large shade tree with a beautiful, fluted, grey trunk and small green leaves that turn butter-yellow in autumn (see also Making a collage of autumnal leaves in a picture frame, page 50). The fruits are three-pointed, leafy, hop-like bracts that each hold a small, nut-like seed.

—

WHERE TO GROW

This tree will tolerate any soil type including clay, chalk and other poor soil conditions. It is extremely versatile and can be grown as a specimen tree, an avenue tree or a hedge – whether clipped (see Creating a standard topiary ball, page 110), pleached (see page 43) or left natural.

HOW TO GROW

Hornbeam is readily available in all tree nurseries and garden centres in every root type from bare-root to root-balled and container-grown as well as being sold as instant hedge plants by specialized growers. There should also be a choice of every nursery stock type from transplants to feathered or standard trees.

GROWING TIP

The wood of hornbeam is very hard, and a pair of sharp, good-quality bypass secateurs is needed to ensure clean cuts and to prevent tearing. This plant makes the perfect hedge grown to any height and is one of the best deciduous species for pleaching and topiary.

Family	Betulaceae
Height	15–25m/50–82ft
Spread	15–20m/50–66ft
Habit	Columnar, spreading or open
Hardiness	Zone 7: <–20°C/–4°F
Position	Full sun or partial shade

NOTABLE CULTIVARS AND OTHER NOTABLE SPECIES

- 'Fastigiata' has an erect pyramidal habit, which is quite narrow when young, broadening out as it matures.
- Rockhampton Red produces good autumn colour with leaves that turn a rich red rather than yellow.
- *C. caroliniana* (American hornbeam) is a small tree very similar in habit to *C. betulus.*

LINGERING LEAVES

Normally in autumn and winter, deciduous trees shed their leaves. However, some trees and hedges that are regularly clipped produce juvenile growth and marcescence, which is the retention of dead leaves through winter until they are pushed off by spring growth. Such juvenility and marcescence are good for a hedge in winter if you want privacy but you do need to clip the hedge regularly.

Indian bean tree

Catalpa bignonioides

Indian bean trees are native in the USA and China, and they have a spreading habit and very large, fleshy leaves. Upright panicles of very showy, orchid-like flowers in late summer are followed by long, green, slender, bean-like seed pods. These turn brown and woody and stay on the tree well into winter.

Family Bignoniaceae	
Height 12–17m/40–56ft	
Spread 12–20m/40–66ft	
Habit Spreading	
Hardiness Zone 6: –20 to –15°C/–4 to 5°F	
Position Full sun	

WHERE TO GROW

This is a tree that can grow wider than its height, so it needs plenty of space to develop to its full potential. Plant in a sheltered part of the garden, as its large leaves can get torn and battered by strong winds. It will grow in most soils that are moist but well-drained and will also tolerate pollution well.

HOW TO GROW

Plant this tree preferably when small and allow it to grow naturally, retaining the lower branches so it forms a broad skirt down to the ground and has lots of character.

GROWING TIP

As the leaves are very fleshy, they are susceptible to late spring frosts especially in the early years after planting. Therefore, protect it with fleece if frosts are forecast, until the tree is well established.

NOTABLE CULTIVAR AND OTHER NOTABLE SPECIES

- 'Aurea' is a golden-leaved form, which will turn green by the time the flowers appear in summer.
- *C. × erubescens* is a lovely hybrid with smaller but more numerous flowers than its parents. 'Purpurea' has young shoots and leaves that are dark purple, almost black, when they appear; it is more popular than the hybrid.
- *C. ovata* (Chinese catalpa) is a small tree to 10m/33ft, with very delicate, cream to pale yellow flowers.
- *C. speciosa* (northern catalpa) is more oval in habit and earlier to flower than *C. bignonioides*.

RUNNER BEANS

The fruits of this tree look like runner beans, and it is where its common name comes from. However, they cannot be eaten for dinner.

Building an ecological log stack

Often as gardeners we are very keen to have a tidy garden and are quick to remove any garden waste such as weeds, fallen leaves and dead branches. This is good for the gardener but not always good for the local biodiversity and it contributes to habitat loss, especially in urban gardens. However, we can still maintain a tidy garden and provide a habitat for fungi, birds, mammals, reptiles and invertebrates by building an ecological log stack in a shady position somewhere in the back of a border or down near the compost heap. This is also another means of disposing of some of our garden waste safely and easily.

The log stack can be any size depending on space, from a single log to several, and every year or two an additional log can be added to the stack as the others begin to rot away. To start it, from broadleaved trees gather some logs or branches, 15–20cm/6–8in in diameter and up to 1m/3ft long. They don't have to be perfectly straight as the odd twists and turns in them will add some character to the finished pile.

Dig some of the logs into the ground to about 50cm/20in below soil level, building a small pyramid resembling organ pipes. This will be a good source of habitat for insects like endangered stag beetles, which need to feed on decaying timber below the ground for 3–7 years during their life cycles. Allow plants to grow over the log stack so they provide shade and cover for foraging mammals and prevent the logs from drying out.

1 Dig a hole 50cm/20in deep and wide enough to hold several logs.
2 Insert a central upright log to start the pyramidal structure.
3 Position and bury more logs and branches around the central log.
4 Finish the log stack pyramid by backfilling soil around the logs to fill in the hole. Now it is ready for beetles to move in.

Katsura

Cercidiphyllum japonicum

Katsura trees are native to China and Japan and are some of the largest temperate trees in Asia, yet they remain medium-sized trees in cultivation. The crown in winter shows the fine delicate branching that is its unmistakeable, unique feature. The young, kidney-shaped leaves emerge bronze, gradually turn to green and then usually colour well in autumn with shades of orange and red (see also Making a collage of autumnal leaves in a picture frame, page 50).

—

WHERE TO GROW

These trees need a moist but well-drained, fertile, acid soil in a sheltered position as, despite being hardy, they are susceptible to late spring frosts, especially when they are young (see Frost damage, page 136). They make perfect solitary specimen trees in any garden with sufficient space.

HOW TO GROW

Katsura is best planted as a container-grown tree (see Planting a tree in a pot for a balcony, page 88). It is usually sold as a feathered tree with branching to the ground, which naturally forms a multi-stemmed tree. However, some nurseries sell it already trained as a standard on a clean trunk. When planted, katsura should be watered in well and not allowed to dry out until established.

GROWING TIP

This tree has very shallow surface roots, which can dry out very quickly, especially in periods of drought. Therefore, apply a 10cm/4in layer of organic mulch over the root plate out to the dripline in order to slow down water lost to evaporation and to keep the roots cool.

Family Cercidiphyllaceae
Height 10–15m/33–50ft
Spread 8m/26ft
Habit Rounded or weeping
Hardiness Zone 5: –15 to –10°C/5 to 14°F
Position Full sun or partial shade

NOTABLE CULTIVARS

- 'Boyd's Dwarf' is a small tree with elegant arching branches, which turn golden orange or yellow in autumn.
- 'Morioka Weeping' is a more upright, weeping form (if that makes sense). Despite its weeping habit, it continues to make height on its own without the need to train it.
- f. *pendulum* is a small to medium-sized tree with weeping branches and a broad crown.

COTTON CANDY
Katsura is sometimes nicknamed the candy floss tree or caramel tree after the smell emitted from the falling leaves in autumn.

Judas tree

Cercis siliquastrum

This ia a small, wide-spreading, deciduous tree with bright pink, pea-like flowers that emerge before the heart-shaped leaves. The flowers can also grow directly off the main trunk and branches, in an adaptation known as cauliflory. They are followed by flattened, deep purple seed pods, which hang vertically from the branches.

—

WHERE TO GROW

Judas trees grow best in fertile, well-drained soils in full sun. Each deserves a special place in the garden to show off its amazing flower display in spring, but will need plenty of space around it to grow to its ultimate size and shape. Do not lose this tree in the back of a border.

HOW TO GROW

These slow-growing trees are available in many forms, from small, bushy, container-grown ones to container-grown standard specimens. Choosing a specimen will depend on availability in the nursery trade, and whether you have time to wait for it to fill its space and to flower.

GROWING TIP

Judas trees do not transplant well and will sit and sulk after planting, so select a small tree with a good root system, which will establish quickly, then leave it to grow without disturbance.

MATTHEW 27:3–5
The common name of Judas tree is derived from the belief that Judas Iscariot hanged himself from this tree after he betrayed Jesus, causing the white flowers to turn blood-red.

Family Fabaceae

Height 8–12m/26–40ft

Spread 8–12m/26–40ft

Habit Spreading

Hardiness Zone 5: –15 to –10°C/5 to 14°F

Position Full sun or partial shade

NOTABLE CULTIVARS AND OTHER NOTABLE SPECIES

- 'Album' (aka f. *albida*) has masses of white flowers along the branches.
- 'Bodnant' bears dark purple flowers along its branches.
- *C. canadensis* (eastern redbud) makes a tree to 10m/33ft tall, with light pink flowers in early summer. 'Forest Pansy' produces ruby-red, heart-shaped leaves that turn to a rich purple-plum during summer.

73

Lawson cypress

Chamaecyparis lawsoniana aka Port Orford cedar

This narrow pyramidal tree develops pendulous branches and drooping leaders, and often has reddish brown, fibrous-barked, multiple trunks. Its aromatic foliage comprises flattened sprays of small, scale-like, glaucous-green leaves.
—

WHERE TO GROW

Lawson cypress prefers full sun and will grow in moist but well-drained acid, neutral or alkaline soil. It makes the perfect solitary specimen in a garden and also looks good when randomly mixed with deciduous trees to make an informal screen along a boundary or as a formally clipped hedging plant.

HOW TO GROW

If Lawson cypress is less than 60cm/24in tall, it can be planted as a bare-root tree. However, if larger than this size, it will need to be root-balled or container-grown to ensure a high success rate of establishment. These conifers are also available as large trees from specialist nurseries.

GROWING TIP

When trimming the foliage of any cypress conifer, it is important not to cut into old wood, as it will not respond and send out new growth from such wood. The best time to prune is in late spring or in late summer.

Family Cupressaceae

Height 45m/147ft

Spread 20m/66ft

Habit Pyramidal

Hardiness Zone 6: −20 to −15°C/−4 to 5°F

Position Full sun

NOTABLE CULTIVARS AND OTHER NOTABLE SPECIES

- 'Columnaris' is a columnar tree with glaucous-blue foliage.
- 'Pendula Vera' is a very graceful weeping form of the species.
- *C. obtusa* (Hinoki cypress) from Japan is a slow-growing tree, to 35m/115ft.
- *C. pisifera* (Sawara cypress) from Japan is another slow-growing conifer, to 35–50m/115–164ft.

CYPRESS, NOT A CEDAR
Port Orford cedar is the North American name for *C. lawsoniana* – the name reflects where it was discovered in Oregon. It was introduced into cultivation in 1854 by collectors working for Charles Lawson, after whom it was named as Lawson cypress in the UK.

Harlequin glorybower

Clerodendrum trichotomum

This small tree is native to China, Korea and Japan and has been grown successfully in gardens since the 1880s. It produces soft downy leaves, which when crushed give off a nutty odour. The fragrant white flowers are set off and housed in maroon calyces in late summer. Harlequin glorybower's fruits begin white and change to bright blue as they mature because of the blue pigment trichotomine, which is where the species name originates.

Family Lamiaceae

Height 3–6m/10–20ft

Spread 3–6m/10–20ft

Habit Spreading or suckering

Hardiness Zone 5: −15 to −10°C/5 to 14°F

Position Full sun or partial shade

WHERE TO GROW

Harlequin glorybower is an easy tree to grow as it will tolerate any soil, providing it is moist but free-draining. Plant in a sheltered part of the garden such as a shrub border; it is not suitable for growing as a specimen isolated in a lawn.

WHAT A CHANCER
Clerodendrum is Greek for 'chance tree'. Take a chance and plant one.

HOW TO GROW

This tree grows to its best as a short standard with low branching. It needs very little formative pruning to maintain its shape.

GROWING TIP

If left to its own devices, harlequin glorybower will sucker freely and when planted in a shrub border will start to take over. Therefore, remove suckers regularly to restrict its movement through the garden (see Suckers and water shoots, page 43).

NOTABLE CULTIVAR

- var. *fargesii* 'Carnival' is a variegated form of the species with creamy white margins on the leaves.

Japanese dogwood
Cornus controversa

An eye-catching plant with its rough-textured trunk and sturdy, upright (surprisingly sharp) fronds, this is not a true palm but part of an ancient group of plants called gymnosperms that date back to the dinosaurs, 65½ million years ago.

—

WHERE TO GROW

Japanese dogwood makes the perfect solitary ornamental specimen tree in the garden at any time of the year, provided it is planted in deep, fertile, free-draining, neutral to acid soil. It also lends itself to being grown by water, to show off by reflection its wonderful form, flowers and autumn berry colour. It is easy to distinguish from any other tree, particularly in winter, because of the tree's growth habit with branches tiered in very distinctive layers. It bears an abundance of clusters of small, creamy white, star-shaped flowers in late spring and early summer along the horizontal branches. Green berries ripen to blue-black in autumn and provide an invaluable food supply for birds.

HOW TO GROW

Most nurseries and garden centres sell Japanese dogwood in a variety of sizes and root systems, both multi-stemmed and on a short single trunk. It's unusual to find several identical trees in appearance as they are grown from seed and they vary considerably. They are characterful trees and should be allowed to grow and take on their own shape and form without any formative pruning. They look good in a garden whatever way they grow.

GROWING TIP

Cornus is prone to sap bleeding or sap leakage, as the sap starts to rise early in spring. Therefore, any pruning should be minimal, light and carried out in midsummer, when in full leaf, or in midwinter, when the tree is fully dormant.

Family	Cornaceae
Height	15m/50ft
Spread	15m/50ft
Habit	Open and layered
Hardiness	Zone 5: −15 to −10°C/5 to 14°F
Position	Full sun

NOTABLE CULTIVARS

- 'Pagoda' has a bushier habit than the species, with wider horizontal branching from the base.
- 'Variegata' is nicknamed the wedding cake tree because of its white-variegated leaves and tiered branches.

NOT FOR THE DOGS
The name dogwood was most probably derived from the Celtic word *dag, dagga* or *dagwood*, which was a small, pointed, wooden tool made from very hard wood and used for cleaning watches and jewellery. The wood of dogwood is very hard and could have been used for this purpose.

Chinese dogwood

Cornus kousa var. *chinensis*

A must for any garden is this small, bushy, vase-shaped tree with its flaking bark on the trunk and larger branches. In late spring or early summer, it produces a profusion of flowers with stunning, large, white bracts, which remain on the tree for several weeks and show pink tinges in the white as they mature. These flowers are followed by small, pink-red, strawberry-like fruits and vivid red-orange autumn leaf colour (see also Making a collage of autumnal leaves in a picture frame, page 50).

WHERE TO GROW

Chinese dogwood grows better when planted in full sun in a sheltered position, but will tolerate partial shade. It needs well-drained, fertile, neutral to acid soil; avoid poor shallow soils.

HOW TO GROW

This tree can be grown as a standard with a clean trunk, or as a multi-stemmed tree (see Creating a multi-stemmed birch, page 66). However, it looks best as a feathered tree with multiple branching from low down to show off the flowers at eye level rather than at the top, where they cannot be seen from the ground.

GROWING TIP

It's best to plant dogwoods as young, small, container-grown plants, which will establish quickly. Then allow them to develop naturally into the shape they decide to make.

Family Cornaceae

Height 4–8m/13–26ft

Spread 4–8m/13–26ft

Habit Vase

Hardiness Zone 6: −20 to −15°C/−4 to 5°F

Position Full sun or partial shade

NOTABLE CULTIVARS AND OTHER NOTABLE SPECIES

- *C. kousa* var. *chinensis* 'China Girl' has whitish green bracts that change to a creamy white.
- *C. kousa* 'Milky Way' develops a broad, fan-shaped crown and has creamy white, pointed bracts.
- *C. kousa* 'Miss Satomi' (aka 'Satomi') produces pink bracts and deep purple autumn colour.
- *C. × elwinortonii* Venus (Venus dogwood) has richly coloured foliage in autumn and strawberry-like fruits (see also Five hardworking trees for any small garden, page 78).

Q. When is a flower not a flower? **A.** When it is a bract (a modified leaf). The flowers on Chinese dogwood are small and inconspicuous, so the four white bracts encircling each flower head are designed to attract insects to the flowers.

Five hardworking trees for any small garden

There is a tree for every setting, and planting the right tree in the right place is an important element of good tree selection and how to get the best out of your garden. With a small garden it is still possible to plant a tree or two, suitable for the available space. If there is room for only a single tree, it's important that you get the most out of it, so it needs to be hardworking with as many seasonal ornamental attributes as possible. Below are five hardworking trees available in the nurseries and garden centres today. For how to plant them see Planting a tree, page 24.

A Ulleung Island rowan
(*Sorbus ulleungensis*)
'Olympic Flame', aka 'Dodong')
Height 4m/13ft
Spread 2m/7ft
Hardiness Zone 6:
–20 to –15°C/–4 to 5°F

This is a deciduous columnar tree native to the island of Ulleung off the South Korean east coast, and it has stout upright branches. The pinnate leaves open bronze, turning a shiny green during summer and to a kaleidoscope of fiery orange and scarlets in autumn. Ulleung rowan has large clusters of creamy white flowers in spring and shiny orange berries into winter.

B Père David's maple
(*Acer davidii* Viper)
Height 4m/13ft
Spread 3m/10ft
Hardiness Zone 5:
–15 to –10°C/5 to 14°F

Viper is an upright form of deciduous Père David's snake-bark maple, which is native to western China. The bark is white and green, striated with red-orange, and resembles a snake's skin. The clusters of flowers in spring ripen to red-brown, winged seeds (samaras), and the dark green leaves turn a delightful brilliant orange in autumn.

C Sargent's cherry
(*Prunus sargentii*)
Height 8–10m/26–33ft
Spread 2–3m/7–10ft
Hardiness Zone 6:
–20 to –15°C/–4 to 5°F

This cherry has an upright, vase-shaped habit, with showy, lens-like, porous cells in the bark, but can be grown as a multi-stemmed tree (see Creating a multi-stemmed birch, page 66). In early spring, it has single pink flowers on bare stems, which last for over three weeks until the leaves open a coppery red before turning green. Sargent's cherry is one of the first trees to display a striking orange-red autumn colour, which will last until wind displaces the foliage (see also Making a collage of autumnal leaves in a picture frame, page 50).

D Venus dogwood
(*Cornus* × *elwinortonii* Venus)
Height 4–8m/13–26ft
Spread 2–4m/7–13ft
Hardiness Zone 5:
–15 to –10°C/5 to 14°F

This hybrid dogwood is a cross between *C. nuttallii* and *C. kousa* var. *chinensis* and makes a small tough tree with large white flower bracts in late spring, possibly the largest bracts of any *Cornus*. The leaves turn a rich yellow, orange and purple in autumn and are offset by strawberry-like fruits.

E Chinese bladdernut
(*Staphylea holocarpa* var. *rosea*)
Height 6m/20ft
Spread 4m/13ft
Hardiness Zone 5:
–15 to –10°C/5 to 14°F

This is a choice plant worthy of any place in the garden. It's often mistaken for a cherry in spring, when it bears its clusters of attractive, pale pink flowers, which are produced in large numbers on mature trees. Chinese bladdernut has bronze leaves in spring and inflated, bladder-like fruit capsules in autumn – from which it gets its common name.

Common hawthorn

Crataegus monogyna aka maythorn, quickthorn

The nicknames of quickthorn and maythorn are because this hawthorn flowers during late spring, when it produces its small, white, fragrant blooms in abundance. They are extremely attractive to many pollinating insects and bees. These flowers develop into small red fruits, known as haws, in autumn, and these are an important food source for wild birds. The trees are also suitable hosts for growing mistletoe (see Establishing mistletoe in a garden tree, page 104).

—

WHERE TO GROW

Hawthorns are very hardy and tolerate a wide range of soils including sand, clay and chalk, but prefer moist but well-drained soil. They do not mind urban pollution and coastal conditions and make perfect trees for a small garden.

HOW TO GROW

This tree can be grown in short standard form as a ornamental specimen tree or in feathered form as a hedging plant in rural locations. It can be pruned hard to encourage new growth to thicken and produce an impenetrable, stock-proof hedge.

GROWING TIP

Whenever pruning, but especially when tackling a hawthorn, be sure to wear good personal protective equipment such as thornproof gloves and suitable eye protection. The many sharp thorns on the twigs are dirty, and when they cut the skin they can leave puncture wounds open to infection. A thorn in the eye would be disastrous.

Family Rosaceae	
Height 4–8m/13–26ft	
Spread 4–8m/13–26ft	
Habit Spreading	
Hardiness Zone 7: <–20°C/–4°F	
Position Full sun or partial shade	

NOTABLE CULTIVAR AND OTHER NOTABLE SPECIES

- 'Stricta' has a columnar habit with upright branches and is useful where space is restricted.
- *C. crus-galli* (cockspur thorn) is a wide-spreading tree, with long thorns, good autumn colour and persistent red berries.
- *C. laevigata* 'Paul's Scarlet', a cultivar of the Midland thorn, is a small rounded tree, with good autumn colour, masses of deep scarlet-pink flowers and small red berries in autumn.
- *C. laevigata* 'Punicea' (aka 'Crimson Cloud') makes a dense spreading tree, with small crimson flowers in spring followed by tiny red berries in autumn.
- *C. persimilis* 'Prunifolia' is a small tree, with dark green leaves turning gold, red and orange in autumn and large red berries.
- *C. persimilis* 'Prunifolia Splendens' develops a broad head and great autumn colour.

Mediterranean cypress

Cupressus sempervirens

The Mediterranean cypress is an iconic, medium-sized evergreen tree of the Mediterranean with a narrow, pencil-shaped habit and scaly bark. It has green, aromatic, scale-like leaves in sprays on upright branches. The round cones are quite large, looking out of place on such an elegant tree.

—

WHERE TO GROW

This versatile tree will grow on most soils from sand to clay, acid to alkaline, in well-drained soil in direct sunshine. Position in a sheltered spot as it loathes strong winds, which can damage the canopy by pulling the upright branches apart.

HOW TO GROW

Regardless of the size, this tree needs to be planted as a container-grown specimen with a good-sized root ball that can support the tree above ground without a need for staking. It makes a perfect solitary tree as a focal point, and is also good when planted in a group to give vertical scale in the garden.

GROWING TIP

Despite its crown being quite narrow and upright, Mediterranean cypress can start to become ungainly as branches get heavy with growth and the large seed cones bend it out of shape, especially on windy sites. To prevent this from happening, wrap the canopy with fine wire, which will soon be lost in the foliage.

Family	Cupressaceae
Height	30m/100ft
Spread	4m/13ft
Habit	Conical
Hardiness	Zone 5: −15 to −10°C/5 to 14°F
Position	Full sun

NOTABLE CULTIVAR AND OTHER NOTABLE SPECIES

- 'Totem' (aka 'Totem Pole') is a very narrow form of the Mediterranean cypress and is suitable for small spaces.
- *C. arizonica* (Arizona cypress) has glaucous blue-green sprays of rounded leaves.
- *C. cashmeriana* (Kashmir cypress) needs a sheltered spot but is the most elegant of all the cypresses, with graceful sprays of pendulous, blue-green foliage.
- *C. macrocarpa* (Monterey cypress) is a parent of the hybrid Leyland cypress (× *Cuprocyparis leylandii*) and makes a large conifer tolerant of seaside winds.

A WHEAT FIELD WITH CYPRESSES

In 1889 Vincent van Gogh painted this scene of a ripe wheat field with a dark fastigiate Provençal cypress towering like a green obelisk to the right and with lighter green olive trees to the left.

Grow your own Christmas tree

Every year during the run-up to Christmas, over 7 million real Christmas trees are cut and sold in the UK to decorate and brighten up our homes, and around 15 million are purchased in the USA. Three types of conifers are grown in plantations for sale: spruce (*Picea*), pine (*Pinus*) and the needle-fast species silver fir (*Abies*). Once planted in plantations, each pine takes around five years to make a saleable size, each spruce seven years and each silver fir ten years. They are grown as a crop specially for Christmas and this may seem a waste, so why not try and grow your own and keep it for each Christmas?

Small, young, container-grown trees are readily available before Christmas in garden centres, nurseries and large DIY stores. Before buying, check that the tree has been grown in a container and has developed a good root system. Avoid any that might have been pulled from the ground and containerized for the festival.

Find a suitable, appropriate-sized container and add plenty of drainage material in the bottom (see Planting a tree in a pot for a balcony, page 88). (In this project I used a pot of 28cm/11in diameter.) Pot it up into a good-quality, soil-based potting compost, such as John Innes No. 3 compost. Cover the compost surface with grit, to reduce water splash. After watering, place the potted tree outdoors in the garden. Allow it to root into the compost and establish.

If there are any over-extended lateral branches unbalancing the tree and making it asymmetrical, they can be pruned back to shape as and when they develop.

When bringing the tree into the house or conservatory, leave it as late as possible – preferably the weekend before Christmas – and keep the tree away from central heating radiators, stoves or open fires. Ensure that it is kept well-watered, but don't be tempted to overwater.

After the festive period, the tree can be taken back into the garden to recuperate and grow a bit more, in readiness for the following Christmas. Like any other pot plant, it will need repotting after consecutive years of growing outdoors.

1 Choose a suitable tree for potting up (here, spruce).
2 Pot it up into a suitable well-drained container with a good-quality, soil-based potting compost, such as John Innes No. 3 compost.
3 Cover the surface of the compost with fine grit. Then water it.
4 Check the tree over before moving it to its final place ready for the festivities and baubles.

Handkerchief tree

Davidia involucrata aka dove tree

This is a tree that certainly lives up to its common name, which is very descriptive and appropriate. As it is very impressive, it will turn heads in spring when the crown looks like it's covered in white handkerchiefs – or white doves roosting on every branch. These are the large bracts of the insignificant, purple-anthered flowers. They are followed by large oval fruits, which hang individually on long stalks.

—

WHERE TO GROW

The handkerchief tree prefers a deep, fertile, moist but well-drained soil in a sheltered position, to give some protection from late spring frosts and strong winds, which will damage the beautiful bracts. It makes the perfect specimen tree in any garden or park.

HOW TO GROW

I often feel that handkerchief tree is miffy and moody because it is not always the easiest to establish. Therefore, it is worth spending a little more money and buying a larger specimen, to guarantee successful establishment. These trees are available as feathered or standard specimens in the nursery, so the choice is yours. You will have to wait at least a decade or two for these trees to flower.

GROWING TIP

A young handkerchief tree can be quite unruly and will try to grow several competitive leaders, so early discipline is important to develop a strong canopy. In summer rather than during the dormant season, prune out some of these leaders with secateurs, to leave one strong one.

Family Nyssaceae
Height 10–15m/33–50ft
Spread 10m/33ft
Habit Spreading
Hardiness Zone 5: −15 to −10°C/5 to 14°F
Position Full sun or partial shade

DAVID'S HANDKERCHIEF
The genus *Davidia* is named after Father Armand David, a French missionary and keen naturalist who travelled in China in the late nineteenth century. He was also known as Père David, and many other plants such as Père David's maple (*Acer davidii* Viper) were also named after him (see Five hardworking trees for any small garden, page 78).

Maidenhair tree

Ginkgo biloba

Maidenhair trees are very long-lived and deciduous, with a symmetrical crown when young, developing to a spreading one with maturity. The easy identification feature is the unique, two-lobed, fan-shaped, green leaf. All maidenhair trees have good, bright yellow autumn colour whatever the cultivar name (see also Making a collage of autumnal leaves in a picture frame, page 50). Their bark is grey and flaky, and they develop yellow, apricot-like fruits, each with a single seed.

WHERE TO GROW

These trees will grow on any soil type – from chalk to acid loam – that is well-drained, providing the site is in full sun. It makes a perfect ornamental specimen in any garden and tolerates urban pollution better than most other trees. See also Planting a tree in a pot for a balcony, page 88.

HOW TO GROW

A maidenhair tree can be bought in a variety of sizes, up to a semi-mature tree, with a root ball or as container-grown plant. Although initially slow – usually taking two or three years to begin to grow after planting – it is fast-growing once established.

GROWING TIP

Maidenhair trees are male or female, and it is impossible to distinguish a tree's sex until it fruits. If possible, you need to buy a cloned male rather than a female tree, as the female fruits contain a compound called butyric acid, which is found in rancid butter and cheese. The flesh of the yellow fruits when ripe smell of vomit or dog faeces, and it is not the aroma that you'll want in the garden in autumn.

Family Ginkgoaceae

Height 20–35m/66–115ft

Spread 10–15m/33–50ft

Habit Columnar when young; then spreading

Hardiness Zone 6: –20 to –15°C/–4 to 5°F

Position Full sun

NOTABLE CULTIVARS

- 'Autumn Gold' (male) is as wide-spreading as it is tall, so needs lots of space.
- 'Blagon' (aka 'Fastigiata Blagon'; non-fruiting) is a columnar tree up to 20m/66ft tall, with upright scaffold and multiple, fine, lateral branches.
- 'Princeton Sentry' (male) is a fast-growing, columnar cultivar.

JURASSIC PARK
This prehistoric tree has been around for a long time; fossils of the maidenhair tree first appear in the early Jurassic epoch, about 201 to 174 million years ago.

87

Planting a tree in a pot for a balcony

There is a tree for every garden situation and, so long as you can provide daylight and water, you can also grow a tree on a balcony or patio. Some trees will naturally restrict their growth to the planting situation, so by planting one of certain species in a container you can suppress its size so that it naturally develops into a bonsai tree while still looking healthy and happy. Good examples are the Persian silk tree (*Albizia julibrissin*) and the maidenhair tree (*Ginkgo biloba*), which comes in many cultivars with different leaf shapes (see page 87).

The best time to plant will be in the dormant period; however, it can be done in the growing season with good aftercare (see page 28). First find a suitable container, preferably a terracotta-type or glazed pot, and a small tree. Place adequate drainage material such as broken terracotta pots (crocks) or washed gravel in the bottom half of the pot; this will prevent waterlogging during wet weather and allow the movement of air to the root system. Then add a layer of good-quality, soil-based potting compost, such as John Innes No. 3 compost, leaving enough space for the root system of the tree.

Place the tree into the compost in the container and top up the compost, firming with your thumbs to the nursery mark, leaving about 2.5cm/1in space just under the rim of the container. Tap the container on the bench to ensure that all the compost has settled to a suitable level and there are no air holes. Finally, to prevent soil splash when watering, add a layer of fine washed gravel to the surface of the pot, then water thoroughly and label the pot.

Through the growing season water the tree regularly, and once a year in spring give a liquid feed of well-balanced fertilizer. You can repot the tree into a larger container after two or three years or give it to a friend to plant in their garden.

1 Half-fill a suitably sized container with drainage material and then some ,loam-based compost, ready to take the depth of the root system of the tree.
2 Place the tree in the centre of the pot with the top of the root ball just below the pot rim.
3 Add more compost and firm evenly to within 2.5cm/1in of the container rim.
4 Add a layer of fine washed gravel, evenly covering the surface of the compost to prevent water splash.
5 Water and label the container.

A This young Persian silk tree (*Albizia julibrissin*) will stay small in this pot, so long as it gets plenty of water and the occasional feed. It will give lots of pleasure to anyone without a garden.

Honey locust

Gleditsia triacanthos

The honey locust is a fast-growing, large tree from eastern North America with an open habit, fine leafing density and deep roots. The flaking bark is brown-grey with shallow fissures, and the branches bear needle-sharp, multiple spines. The compound pinnate leaves are green, turning to a wonderful golden yellow in autumn (see also Making a collage of autumnal leaves in a picture frame, page 50). After flowering, the honey locust develops long, shiny, brown-red seed pods, which stay on the tree throughout winter and rattle in the wind.

—

WHERE TO GROW

This is a drought-resistant tree suitable for most acid to neutral soil types, providing they are well-drained and in full sun. It will even grow in poor infertile soils, and it tolerates urban atmospheric pollution.

HOW TO GROW

Like other legumes, honey locust has deep roots, so a container-grown tree will establish quickly. Because of its light crown density, it will cast little shade on to the garden so is suitable for planting in a border.

GROWING TIP

Be sure to plant this tree away from footpaths or where there is regular foot traffic, and raise the crown/skirt high enough for passers-by to avoid puncture wounds from the dangerous thorns. Otherwise, you could opt for the thornless form.

SWEET AS HONEY
The common name honey locust originates from the sweet taste of the legume pulp in the seed pods, which was used for food and traditional medicine by native American peoples.

Family Fabaceae	
Height 20m/66ft	
Spread 8m/26ft	
Habit Open or oval	
Hardiness Zone 6: −20 to −15°C/−4 to 5°F	
Position Full sun	

NOTABLE FORM AND CULTIVAR

- f. *inermis* is a form of honey locust without any thorns, making it a good selection where there are children in the vicinity.
- f. *inermis* 'Sunburst' is a medium-sized tree developing golden yellow leaves in summer.

New Zealand lacebark

Hoheria sexstylosa

This graceful evergreen tree is native to New Zealand and is an upright grower when juvenile and a 'weeper' when mature. It has leathery, sharp-toothed, glossy leaves as well as large, fragrant, white flowers in summer, which develop into winged dry fruit. There are only six species in this genus and they are still uncommon in gardens in the northern hemisphere and should be planted more.

WHERE TO GROW

It was thought that this plant was tender and subject to frosts, but it has in fact proven frost hardy provided it is grown in a sheltered spot in the garden and not subjected to cold winds. It will grow in any fertile, well-drained, neutral to acid soil, but will not succeed on clay. New Zealand lacebark is also a good tree for planting by the seaside.

HOW TO GROW

As this is an elegant evergreen, it makes a good screen or hedge plant. It also looks good at the back of a herbaceous border or as a single ornamental specimen. It can be grown naturally without any intervention or else be clipped to shape.

GROWING TIP

Although the New Zealand lacebark is frost hardy, its performance will be improved if it is planted in front of a sunny wall. Plant in late spring or early summer, after the threat of frost has disappeared.

A TREE WITH STYLE – SIX STYLES
The species name *sexstylosa* is Latin for 'six styles'. These form part of the beautiful white flowers.

Family Malvaceae

Height 8m/26ft

Spread 6m/20ft

Habit Columnar when young; weeping with maturity

Hardiness Zone 4: −10 to −5°C/14 to 23°F

Position Full sun or partial shade

NOTABLE CULTIVARS AND OTHER SPECIES

- 'Snow White' has a pyramidal habit, and masses of white flowers in summer.
- 'Stardust' is a columnar tree with fragrant white flowers in late summer.
- *H. angustifolia* has narrow, grey-green to dark green, evergreen leaves, and white flowers.
- *H.* 'Glory of Amlwch' is a semi-evergreen hybrid between *H. glabrata* and *H. sexstylosa*, with pure white flowers.
- *H. lyallii* has hairy deciduous leaves and slightly scented, white flowers in summer.
- *H. populnea* is the tallest-growing lacebark, making an evergreen tree to 12m/40ft high.

Black walnut

Juglans nigra

Black walnut is a handsome, fast-growing, deciduous tree native to eastern North America and was introduced to European gardens in 1629. It is a large shade tree with deeply furrowed, black bark – even when juvenile – and large pinnate leaves with 10–12 toothed leaflets, which have a strong smell when crushed. The fruits are large and round in pairs and contain an edible nut.

—

WHERE TO GROW

This tree grows to its full potential in deep, fertile, moist but free-draining soil, and it will tolerate any soil type from acid to alkaline. It is a large tree needing lots of sunshine and plenty of space to develop its wide crown, and it makes one of the best park trees or specimen ones in a large garden.

HOW TO GROW

Like many of the trees in the family Juglandaceae, walnuts produce a taproot and do not like it being disturbed. Therefore, it is important to plant small container-grown trees for optimum establishment.

GROWING TIP

Black walnuts are the tree of choice in areas prone to late spring frosts (see Frost damage, page 136), but in warmer regions the common or English walnut (*J. regia*) might well be more suitable.

Family	Juglandaceae
Height	20–30m/66–100ft
Spread	10–20m/33–66ft
Habit	Rounded or open
Hardiness	Zone 6: –20 to –15°C/–4 to 5°F
Position	Full sun

ALLELOPATHIC
All walnuts produce a chemical called juglone, which deters any other trees from growing near it. Such allelopathy prevents competition and so enhances each walnut tree's chances of thriving.

OTHER NOTABLE SPECIES AND CULTIVARS

- *J. ailantifolia* (Japanese walnut) bears large pinnate leaves.
- *J. mandshurica* (aka *J. cathayensis*; Chinese walnut) is naturally multi-stemmed, with long pinnate leaves.
- *J. regia* (common or English walnut) has a broad round crown and smooth bark; it produces a good crop of edible nuts if you can beat the squirrels to them. 'Broadview' makes a compact, medium-sized tree and is the best cropping cultivar.

Golden chain tree

Laburnum anagyroides

This small deciduous tree has thin, smooth, dark green bark. Its spreading main branches are pendulous at the ends and have hairy twigs bearing dark green, trifoliate leaves with long leaf stalks. The flowers are the main ornamental feature of this tree in late spring; they are in long, pendent, golden yellow, pea-like, scented racemes. These develop into leguminous pods holding small black seeds, which are highly poisonous to humans and animals.

—

WHERE TO GROW

Laburnum needs full sun and will not tolerate shade. Plant in fertile, very well-drained soil. It will stand seaside winds with some shelter and is most suitable for the small garden as a solitary specimen, in a border or in a lawn, or when grown over a frame to highlight the pendent flowers. Always keep this tree well away from children and animals, and also educate children about their toxicity.

HOW TO GROW

This is best planted as a container-grown, small tree from a young age rather than transplanted as a large tree, because the root system never really catches up with the top growth and it may therefore fall over or lean as it grows.

GROWING TIP

Laburnum requires minimal pruning and will flower well without any such intervention. If you need to do some formative pruning, such as removing crossing branches or lifting the lower branches, carry it out when the tree is fully dormant or in midsummer when the tree is in full leaf, to prevent sap bleeding.

Family	Fabaceae
Height	7m/23ft
Spread	2m/7ft
Habit	Spreading
Hardiness	Zone 6: −20 to −15°C/−4 to 5°F
Position	Full sun

NOTABLE CULTIVAR AND HYBRIDS

- 'Yellow Rocket' is a narrowly oval tree, with pale yellow flowers.
- *L. × watereri* 'Vossii' has very long, trailing racemes of bright yellow flowers.
- + *Laburnocytisus adami* (aka 'Adamii'; Adam's laburnum) is a small graft hybrid between laburnum and purple broom, and produces three different types of flowers on the same branches.

THE LORD OF THE RINGS

J.R.R. Tolkien may have been inspired by the laburnum for the creation of Laurelin, the gold tree, one of the mythological Two Trees of Valinor in *The Silmarillion*.

Making a bee hotel

There is a big push to be more environmentally friendly in the garden when it comes to pest control, and most gardeners now want to adopt an organic approach wherever possible. Solitary bees are a good example of an insect that will help with flower pollination, while lacewings feed on aphids, so any encouragement that you can give them will be useful. Solitary bees need somewhere to nest, as unlike honeybees they do not live in a hive with a queen; instead, they each make a nest by boring into a piece of wood or stone and creating a small nursery, where they lay their fertilized eggs.

There are many pre-made bee hotels available to buy in garden centres and retail outlets, but it's more exciting to make your own, which will be almost free apart from a little of your time. You can make a bee hotel as large or small as you wish – and as elaborate – but to a certain extent its size does depend on the space that you have available to place one. It is important to site it in a suitably sheltered position, where it is warm and dry on a sunny wall of the house or garden shed, and easy for the bees to find. Once it's erected you will spend hours watching the bees visit it, laying their eggs and sealing the ends with mud; it is very therapeutic.

YOU WILL NEED

- Sawn timber, 14cm/5½in wide by 2cm/¾in thick
- Marine ply, 3mm/⅛in thick (for back)
- Saw and secateurs
- Electric drill
- Exterior wood glue
- Wood screws (5.0 × 50mm/ 10 gauge × 2in) and screwdriver
- 2 or 3 picture-plate hangers (depending on the weight of the completed hotel)
- Sections of small branches
- Hollow bamboo canes of varying sizes

1 Build the frame about the size of a bird box by cutting the timber into five short lengths. The size will depend on how much space you have available for the final bee hotel. Drill, glue and screw these lengths together to make a square box with a sloping roof and fix a back to the box to keep it cosy. Attach the picture-plate hangers to the back of the frame.

2 Cut the small branches and the bamboo canes to length to fit the box, slicing the canes between nodes to allow easy entry for the bees. Ensure that the ends are smooth with no splinters that can potentially damage the bees when they go into the hotel. Drill the ends of the branches with several holes of different diameters (4mm/⅛in, 6mm/¼in and 8mm/⅓in) as deep as possible without breaking through to the other end. Then remove the pith from the bamboo canes.

3 Arrange these canes and one or two branches in the box so that they are all tightly held and unlikely to fall out if disturbed.

4 Find a suitable position on a sunny wall and secure the box to the wall with the picture-plate hangers.

5 Sit back and wait for the first tenants to arrive at the hotel.

Sweetgum

Liquidambar styraciflua

This medium-sized to large tree introduced into gardens from the eastern states in the USA in the seventeenth century is one of the most popular trees for stunning, sensational, long-lasting ornamental autumn colour (see also Making a collage of autumnal leaves in a picture frame, page 50). It will always perform year in, year out, especially if some of the named clones are selected and planted. The leaves are similar to a maple (*Acer*), but are arranged alternately along the stems, whereas those of maples are set opposite each other.

—

WHERE TO GROW

Sweetgum will grow in most fertile, neutral to acid, moist soils providing they are well-drained, but it will not tolerate chalk. It makes the perfect specimen ornamental tree in any garden, and is ideal for use as an avenue tree. Plant in full sun for the best autumn colour effects.

HOW TO GROW

Trees are available in a variety of shapes and forms, from feathered trees to standards in many different sizes. Sweetgum transplants and establishes well, and is a reliable tree.

GROWING TIP

Do not be alarmed by any corky bark wings on the young stems and branches. This is a typical attribute of these trees, and some of them demonstrate it more than others.

Family Altingiaceae	
Height 12–30m/40–100ft	
Spread 8m/26ft	
Habit Pyramidal when young; rounded with maturity	
Hardiness Zone 6: −20 to −15°C/−4 to 5°F	
Position Full sun	

NOTABLE CULTIVARS

- 'Lane Roberts' has an open pyramidal crown and autumn foliage of an intense dark red to black-red colour.
- 'Palo Alto' is a pyramidal form, to 20m/66ft tall, with corky stems and orange-red to deep purple leaves in autumn.
- 'Stella' (aka 'Stared') has a pyramidal habit and deeply cut, star-like leaves with good autumn colour.
- 'Worplesdon' is the most popular cultivar in the UK, with upright branching in a pyramidal crown and is reliably stunning in autumn.

IT'S ALL IN A WORD

Liquidambar is from the Latin *Liquidus ambar*. A liquid aromatic balsam is obtained from liquidambar trees and is used for perfumes and medicine.

Tulip tree

Liriodendron tulipifera aka yellow poplar

The tulip tree is a large, fast-growing tree from the eastern USA with very distinctive, shiny green, lobed leaves, which turn butter-yellow in autumn (see also Making a collage of autumnal leaves in a picture frame, page 50). Green, tulip-shaped flowers with orange markings appear in early summer.

WHERE TO GROW
This tree needs plenty of space to develop to its full potential. It is best suited to a very large garden or when grown as a specimen in a paddock or parkland setting. It prefers a moist but free-draining, fertile soil.

HOW TO GROW
Tulip tree is usually grown as a standard, as it wants to go up quickly and will make a very large shade tree. It can be planted at any size, from a small standard to a large, semi-mature tree, but should preferably have been container-grown in the nursery or have a well-established root ball.

GROWING TIP
Especially during periods of dry weather, be sure to give your young tree plenty of water during the first few years after planting, until it is independent and well-established.

Family Magnoliaceae

Height 40m/130ft

Spread 15m/50ft

Habit Oval or open

Hardiness Zone 6: −20 to −15°C/−4 to 5°F

Position Full sun

NOTABLE CULTIVARS AND ANOTHER NOTABLE SPECIES

- 'Aureomarginatum' is a beautiful cultivar, with bright yellow variegation on the edge of each leaf.
- 'Fastigiatum' is an upright form, with a broadly columnar habit; it can flower earlier in its life than the species.
- *L. chinense* is the Chinese version of the tulip tree with larger, more deeply lobed leaves, which are silver-blue on the undersides.

UNRELATED TO BULBS
The similarity of the flower shape on this tree to that of the tulip bulb gave it the common name of tulip tree. Its fluttering leaves resemble those of a poplar (*Populus*), hence its other common name, yellow poplar.

Bullbay

Magnolia grandiflora aka loblolly magnolia

Introduced to Europe from the southern states of the USA in 1734, this is one of the most popular evergreen magnolias that we grow in gardens today, with several cultivars available in the nurseries. It is a tough grower and provides extra-large, heavily scented, creamy white, cup-shaped flowers in summer and early autumn.

—

WHERE TO GROW

Some people may deem this tree to be a tender wall shrub because it is habitually grown against a sunny wall to provide some form of winter protection, yet it is very hardy and will flourish as a free-standing tree on any moist but well-drained, acidic soil. If the soil is deep fertile loam, bullbay will even tolerate some chalk.

HOW TO GROW

Plant this tree with some form of root ball – grown either in the field or in a container – in spring or autumn for successful establishment; avoid bare-root trees. Bullbay is usually available as a feathered standard with branching to the ground or as a standard with a clear stem. Your choice will depend on where it will be grown.

GROWING TIP

Because bullbays are slow-growing until they become established, prune them in spring, before they start to grow, rather than in summer, which is the standard recommendation for evergreen trees.

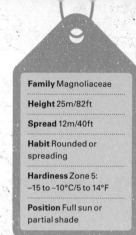

Family Magnoliaceae
Height 25m/82ft
Spread 12m/40ft
Habit Rounded or spreading
Hardiness Zone 5: −15 to −10°C/5 to 14°F
Position Full sun or partial shade

FUNICULAR RAILWAYS
The bright orange seeds on magnolias are attached to the bright red carpels (on the seed head) by fine threads called funicles, which is how some railway carriages are attached to a cable, hence the name.

NOTABLE CULTIVARS AND OTHER NOTABLE SPECIES

- 'Exmouth' bears shiny leaves and very large, richly scented flowers.
- 'Galissonnière' is a very hardy form, producing large, shiny green leaves with bronze fine hairs underneath.
- 'Goliath' has short glossy leaves and very large flowers, which it produces earlier than the species.
- *M. delavayi*, from China, has large, dull green leaves and fragrant, creamy white flowers from summer through to autumn.
- *M. virginiana* (sweet bay) is semi-evergreen in a mild-temperate winter, with small, creamy white flowers in summer.

Saucer magnolia

Magnolia × soulangeana

There are many deciduous species and cultivars of magnolias available to plant in a garden, and your personal preference of flower colour and size and shape will determine which one is chosen. However, a commonly planted, reliable one is *M. × soulangeana*, which carries many showy, saucer-shaped flowers in spring, in varying colours including white, pink and purple.

Family Magnoliaceae	
Height 4–8m/13–26ft	
Spread 4–8m/13–26ft	
Habit Spreading	
Hardiness Zone 6: −20 to −15°C/−4 to 5°F	
Position Full sun or partial shade	

WHERE TO GROW
Saucer magnolias prefer a fertile, moist but well-drained, acid or neutral soil. Because of their natural shape and size they are perfect solitary specimens in a border or in a lawn.

HOW TO GROW
Purchase these trees as container-grown plants as they are quite fussy if their fleshy roots are disturbed. When buying a young magnolia tree, opt for a reputable nursery that will look after the root systems in winter, because a hard frost can kill magnolia roots in a pot.

GROWING TIP
Because of their fleshy roots, you should firm in a magnolia tree with your fists instead of your heel when planting, so you can judge the pressure on the root area better and you do not accidentally damage the roots and check their growth for a while. After backfilling, water in the tree well.

OTHER NOTABLE SPECIES AND CULTIVARS

- *M. campbellii* is a large tree and one of the first magnolias to flower, producing large dark pink flowers from late winter.
- *M.* 'Elizabeth' bears pale yellow, cup-shaped flowers in spring.
- *M. kobus* makes a large tree, with small white flowers in spring.
- *M.* 'Star Wars' carries fragrant, rosy pink flowers from mid- to late spring.

LET IT BEE
Magnolias are a group of ancient plants, arriving on Earth before bees, so evolved to be pollinated by beetles instead.

Siberian crab apple

Malus baccata

The crab apples are small to medium-sized trees with varying heights and habits, but most are spreading. They all have showy flowers in spring followed by ornamental fruits, and some develop good autumn colour. The Siberian crab is always the first to flower, displaying its fragrant, virgin-white blooms usually before the leaves emerge or as they do so. They are followed by small, yellow-red fruits and are also suitable host trees for growing mistletoe (see Establishing mistletoe in a garden tree, page 104).

—

WHERE TO GROW

These trees will grow in any moist but well-drained, fertile soil with a neutral pH; they will not tolerate waterlogged conditions. Because of their small size, they are perfect candidates for a small garden and make beautiful, hard-working specimen trees showing some form of ornamental attribute throughout the year. They also provide a much-needed food source for honeybees during the flowering period.

HOW TO GROW

Plant crab apples when the trees are small. Then allow them to develop their crowns with little or no intervention from secateurs, unless a crown needs balancing because of overextended branches. Most of these trees are grafted, so watch out for suckers from the rootstock and remove them as soon as they are spotted (see Suckers and water shoots, page 43).

GROWING TIP

Siberian crabs are prone to a fungal infection called apple scab. The symptoms appear in late spring as dark blotches on the leaves, which turn yellow and fall prematurely in summer. Rake up the leaves and burn them, to control the disease organically.

Family	Rosaceae
Height	6–10m/20–33ft
Spread	6–10m/20–33ft
Habit	Spreading
Hardiness	Zone 6: –20 to –15°C/–4 to 5°F
Position	Full sun

NOTABLE CULTIVARS AND OTHER NOTABLE SPECIES

There so many good species and cultivars for the small garden – too numerous to mention – so below is a selection of popular ones that merit planting.

- 'Gracilis' is a broad weeping tree to a height of 4–6m/13–20ft, with small white flowers in late spring.
- *M.* 'Evereste' has flowers that start red in bud and open white with a hint of pink. The small fruits stay on the tree for a long period until they are removed by the birds.
- *M.* × *floribunda* (Japanese crab apple) is a tree with long arching branches, flowering early with crimson buds opening to pale pink flowers, followed by small, red and yellow fruits.
- *M.* 'John Downie' is an old spreading cultivar with large, bright red and orange fruits.
- *M.* × *moerlandsii* 'Profusion' bears young, copper-coloured leaves followed by a profusion of rich purple flowers, then small, blood-red fruits.
- *M.* 'Royalty' produces rich purple leaves, crimson flowers and dark red fruits.
- *M. toringo* is a flowering Japanese crab with a weeping habit and pink-budded flowers that open white, followed by small, red or yellow fruits.
- *M.* × *zumi* 'Golden Hornet' has white flowers followed by persistent yellow fruits.

Malus prattii

LOVE AND MARRIAGE
It was once said that if you throw the pips of a crab apple into the fire while saying the name of your love, and the pips then explode, the love is true.

Malus × *floribunda*

Establishing mistletoe in a garden tree

In some traditions, mistletoe is used to decorate a house at Christmastime and a kiss is shared beneath it. Well, why not join in the festive fun and even try growing your own on a tree in your garden?

The common European mistletoe is a hemiparasite called *Viscum album* while the North American mistletoe is *Phoradendron leucarpum*. Both have a preference for host trees in the Rosaceae family including hawthorn (*Crataegus*) and apple (*Malus*) as well as other species such as lime (*Tilia*), poplar (*Populus*) and *Robinia*. The mistletoe will root beneath the bark of these trees and draw water and nutrients from them, but, unlike a true parasite, it can also photosynthesize through its green leaves and make its own energy, so it needs a sunny spot on the tree.

Mistletoe is dioecious, which means the male and female flowers are on two separate plants, so you need to find a female mistletoe plant in fruit, to collect the fertile fruits. If that's not possible, wait to source the fruits until Christmastime, when there may be lots of mistletoe available.

The best time to carry out the seed sowing is mid- to late winter. Squash the white translucent fruits with your fingers to extract the seeds, but leave some of a sticky substance called viscin on the seeds to act as a natural sticking agent. Rub the seeds on to the bark of the younger branches of the healthy host tree, letting the viscin dry so sticking the seeds to the bark, where they will germinate and grow. This is mimicking what a bird would do in nature by eating the fruit and pooing it out on to a branch. Mark the branches with a ribbon or label to remember where the seed sowing took place. Then stand back and be patient – this is a long-term investment.

In early spring, check for signs of germination, which would look like small leafless stems growing out of the bark from where the seeds were planted. Mistletoe is slow-growing in its early years, and it will take four to five years for establish, and a bit longer before you will be able harvest it for Christmas.

1 Collect the fresh mistletoe fruits with the seeds inside.
2 Choose a suitable host branch and squash the fruits, rubbing them gently into the bark on the branch.
3 The young mistletoe seeds will germinate, and the seedlings start growing in the branch.

A This mature lime tree (*Tilia*) is covered in well-established mistletoe.

Dawn redwood

Metasequoia glyptostroboides

As it was discovered in western China in only 1941, this is a relatively new tree in the horticultural world, but it is now – rightly – one of the most commonly planted trees globally. It is the most charming and charismatic deciduous conifer in the garden. It makes the perfect pyramidal shape with fine, lime-green, linear needles, which turn copper-brown in autumn before dropping. The trunk is flared at the base and fluted with reddish brown, stringy bark.

—

WHERE TO GROW

The dawn redwood will grow on most acid or alkaline soils providing they are well-drained. It makes an ideal solitary specimen in a lawn or border, and looks good when planted in a group beside water, for its reflection on bright autumn and winter days.

HOW TO GROW

These trees are available in many sizes, but they grow fast once in the ground, so there is no need to buy too large a specimen. Plant a container-grown, feathered young tree with a canopy to the ground and then raise its skirt as required, to show off the attractive bark, but don't lift the skirt too high.

GROWING TIP

A seed-raised dawn redwood will develop a fluted trunk as it matures, while specimens grown from cuttings usually have smooth unfluted trunks. Nurserymen will know how their trees were grown.

Family	Cupressaceae
Height	25–30m/82–100ft
Spread	8m/26ft
Habit	Pyramidal
Hardiness	Zone 7: <–20°C/–4°F
Position	Full sun

NOTABLE CULTIVAR AND ANOTHER DECIDUOUS CONIFER

- Gold Rush is the golden form of the species, and it retains its colouring through the summer.
- *Taxodium distichum* (swamp cypress) from the USA is a deciduous conifer with an irregular crown and good autumn colour; it is tolerant of any soil condition.

NOT SO NEW NOW
For many years this was one of the latest introductions into our gardens, but in 1994 David Noble rediscovered the Wollemi pine (*Wollemia nobilis*) growing in a deep gorge in Australia, and it became the new tree on the block in gardens.

Black mulberry

Morus nigra

This medium-sized, long-lived tree is thought to have been introduced to the rest of Europe by the Romans. It makes a wonderful, gnarled, architectural specimen, usually leaning and full of character with age (see also Researching and finding an old veteran tree, page 124). The bark is pale brown in colour and rugged, while the heart-shaped leaves are rough on top and downy beneath. Its very tart, dark purple fruit is highly valued, especially in pies or ice cream or as a botanical in gin.

Family Moraceae	
Height 8–12m/26–40ft	
Spread 8–12m/26–40ft	
Habit Rounded or spreading	
Hardiness Zone 6: –20 to –15°C/–4 to 5°F	
Position Full sun or partial shade	

WHERE TO GROW

It will grow in moist but well-drained soil of any pH, but prefers a deep fertile soil and full sun to ripen the fruit. A black mulberry tree needs plenty of space, as once fully established it will grow quite fast.

HOW TO GROW

Black mulberries are self-fertile and are best planted as small, container-grown, feathered trees, or as multi-stemmed ones. They are difficult to train to a formal shape, and every tree will take on a different shape and form, which is what is so nice about planting one.

GROWING TIP

Prune this tree during the dormant season or when it is in full leaf, as at other times the pruning wounds will bleed and weep a sticky white latex, which can be quite messy.

IT'S NEVER BLACK AND WHITE
The black mulberry was introduced in the seventeenth century by King James VI and I, to be planted as a food source for the silkworm. However, it was unsuccessful as silkworms prefer the white mulberry.

NOTABLE CULTIVARS AND ANOTHER NOTABLE SPECIES

- 'Chelsea' (aka 'King James') produces large succulent fruits with a very rich flavour; it has historical interest as it was first noticed at Chelsea Physic Garden in London.
- 'Wellington' is a heavy cropper bearing medium-sized fruits with a good flavour.
- *M. alba* (white mulberry) is grown for its large leaves. The fruits are white with a hint of pink and not as tasty as those of black mulberry.

Black tupelo

Nyssa sylvatica

The black tupelo is a medium-sized tree with small, glossy green leaves turning a brilliant dark red, orange and yellow in autumn (see also Making a collage of autumnal leaves in a picture frame, page 50). The fruits are small, fleshy and black-blue in early autumn, and are held on long stalks in clusters of one to three. It can be slow to establish and will need plenty of formative pruning to encourage and maintain a good shape.

—

WHERE TO GROW

This tree prefers a deep, moist, acid, loamy soil, preferably adjacent to water, as it grows in marshy conditions in its native habitat in the eastern regions of the USA. Its reflection in any water will exaggerate its colours on a sunny autumnal day.

HOW TO GROW

Black tulepo has a habit of losing its dominant leader very early in its life, making a bushy tree, so early formative pruning (see page 42) is important to ensure a strong-growing specimen.

GROWING TIP

Plant as a small container-grown tree, as black tulepo has a deep taproot and does not transplant well. Therefore, only a few specialist nurseries will sell it. After planting, keep especially well-watered until established.

NOTABLE CULTIVARS AND ANOTHER NOTABLE SPECIES

- 'Sheffield Park' is a clone selected from the trees growing by the lake at Sheffield Park, UK.
- 'Wildfire' produces new foliage that is orange-red to red, and in autumn it turns an even fierier red.
- 'Wisley Bonfire' has a slightly broader crown when young and the most incredible autumn colour.
- *N. sinensis* (Chinese tupelo), to 10m/33ft tall and wide, is from China and usually has several stems. It is better-behaved in its growth habit than *N. sylvatica* and has very good autumn colour as it gets older; a good cultivar is 'Jim Russell'.

Family Nyssaceae	
Height 20–25m/66–82ft	
Spread 6–9m/20–30ft	
Habit Generally pyramidal when young; becoming rounded with age	
Hardiness Zone 6: –20 to –15°C/–4 to 5°F	
Position Full sun or partial shade	

BONFIRE NIGHT
This is a tree that will set any garden on fire with its brilliant autumnal tints, especially the cultivar 'Wisley Bonfire'.

Olive

Olea europaea

Olives are small evergreen trees with small, grey-green, leathery leaves and small, fragrant, white, feathery flowers in summer. They are long-lived – some of the oldest trees being 2,000 years old. At one time, it was fashionable to plant an old gnarled specimen rescued from an olive grove, to add character and age to a garden, but with the increasing threats of biosecurity, and in particular a disease called *Xylella* (see page 136), this idea has fallen out of favour with landscape designers . . . thank goodness.

—

WHERE TO GROW

Some people imagine that a Mediterannean tree such as an olive doesn't like cold. However, it will tolerate temperatures down to –10°C/14°F provided it is planted in full sun and not subjected to prolonged low temperatures. In the garden, olive trees need deep, fertile, well-drained soil. For those to be grown in a container, use a soil-based compost and plenty of drainage material in the bottom of the pot (see also Planting a tree in a pot for a balcony, page 88).

HOW TO GROW

Most olives are grown as half-standards in the classical Tuscan form (with a short trunk about 1m/3ft tall) or as a full standard (with a trunk 1.5–1.8m/5–6ft tall). They can also be trained as multi-stemmed trees in the garden (see Creating a multi-stemmed birch, page 66) and as topiary (see Creating a standard topiary ball, page 110).

GROWING TIP

If you are thinking of growing olives as a crop as well as an ornamental, you will need to plant a pollinator such as 'Pendolino' or 'Maurino' in the garden as some olive trees are not self-fertile.

Family	Oleaceae
Height	4–8m/13–26ft
Spread	2–3m/7–10ft
Habit	Vase or rounded
Hardiness	Zone 4: –10 to –5°C/14 to 23°F
Position	Full sun

NOTABLE CULTIVARS

- 'Frantoio' (self-fertile) is a Tuscan cultivar, grown as an ornamental, but also with the potential to be a good fruiting tree.
- 'Leccino' (self-fertile) is another Tuscan cultivar, which can produce black olives and high-quality olive oil.

RAMUM OLIVAE
An olive branch held by a dove was deemed a Christian symbol of peace in the fifth century and again in the eighteenth century in Britain and America.

Creating a standard topiary ball

Topiary is the art of training plants, usually evergreens, into different shapes and forms as ornamental features in the garden. It can take several years to train a plant into the desired shape, and once completed it will require regular clipping to maintain and possibly improve the shape. There are various evergreens that are suitable for topiary, including yew (*Taxus baccata*), box (*Buxus sempervirens*), bay laurel (*Laurus nobilis*), Japanese holly (*Ilex crenata*) and Delavay privet (*Ligustrum delavayanum*). Deciduous trees that also topiarize well are beech (*Fagus sylvatica*), field maple (*Acer campestre*) and hornbeam (*Carpinus betulus*).

There are standard topiary forms, such as balls, cubes, pyramids, spirals, standard balls and pom-poms or cloud trees, in a range of sizes available to buy online and in garden centres. However, it's always fun to create your own for your garden, and you'll save a lot of money.

You will need a young plant that is suitable for clipping and training. Either plant it in the ground in its final position or containerize it (see Planting a tree in a pot for a balcony, page 88) until finally trained into a topiary shape and then find a spot in the garden. Feed it well with a well-balanced fertilizer to encourage lots of fresh vigorous growth.

Decide what shape you would like to create with your plant and begin training it. Here, I have trained a bay laurel into a standard ball, which is a ball on a trunk. Select a single stem and remove the leaves and lateral branches from the stem, to give a clean trunk. Once the desired height is reached, start to clip the growth at the top of the stem into the shape of a ball. There's a saying 'measure twice, cut once' and that's what you need to do to get a neat, well-balanced form.

Carry out this process over several years to produce a tight ball to the diameter required. You will need a little patience to get to the end result, but when you do you may want to move on to a more complicated shape, like a spiral or a peacock.

1 Visit your local nursery or garden centre and buy a young healthy plant (here, bay laurel) ready to be containerized.
2 Select a vigorous stem and prune off any leaves or small branches.
3 Once the required height is reached, clip the top growth into a ball.
4 Continue to shape your young plant. Here are a selection of topiary bay laurel shapes: (left to right) a pyramidal cone, a small standard spiral ball and a mature standard ball.

Tibetan cherry

Prunus serrula

This tree from western China is one of most ornamental cherries in the garden, but unlike most cherries it is grown for its bark effect throughout the year and not for its flowers, which are white and small in spring. Even on young trees, it bears shiny, peeling, mahogany-copper bark that resembles a piece of French-polished furniture and lights up the garden on any sunny day. The leaves are small, casting no shade beneath the canopy but providing some good autumn colour (see also Making a collage of autumnal leaves in a picture frame, page 50).

WHERE TO GROW

Tibetan cherry prefers any deep fertile soil that is moist but well-drained in a sunny part of the garden. It makes the perfect ornamental, solitary specimen in a shrub or herbaceous border or in the lawn, where the peeling shiny bark will be highlighted by direct sunshine.

HOW.TO GROW

This tree is available in nurseries as a standard or multi-stemmed plant in various sizes, and as container-grown or root-balled. Plant a small tree without a stake, as staking can damage or mark the bark on the main trunk, which is the attribute to show off.

GROWING TIP

Tibetan cherry will send out small thin side shoots on the main trunk, which – if left too late before being removed – will disfigure the bark effect. Therefore, rub them off with the thumb as soon as possible after they appear, or else prune them off with secateurs (see also How to prune trees, page 39).

Family	Rosaceae
Height	6–10m/20–33ft
Spread	5m/16ft
Habit	Vase
Hardiness	Zone 6: –20 to –15°C/–4 to 5°F
Position	Full sun

ANOTHER NOTABLE SPECIES

- *P. maackii* (Manchurian cherry) is another medium-sized cherry, to 8–12m/26–40ft, with good ornamental bark. 'Amber Beauty' is a charming cultivar with beautiful, peeling, shiny golden bark.

CHINESE WILSON

Tibetan cherry was introduced into cultivation from western Sichuan in 1908 by Ernest Henry Wilson, who worked for the Royal Botanic Gardens, Kew, UK and the Arnold Arboretum in Boston, Massachusetts, USA.

Yoshino cherry

Prunus × yedoensis

One of the best of the flowering cherries is the Yoshino cherry, which was introduced from Japan to the West in 1907. It is one of the most prolific flowering Japanese cherries, with little room for leaves once in flower from early to late spring. Its habit is vase-shaped in its early years and then it begins to produce a spreading crown, becoming wider than its height. The flowers are single, blush-white and are followed by dark green leaves, which turn yellow in autumn.

WHERE TO GROW

This cherry will tolerate most soil types, including chalk and clay, but does not like shallow or waterlogged soils. Therefore, for the best flowering and autumn colour, plant in full sun and well-drained soil.

HOW TO GROW

There is a place in many small gardens for flowering cherries as single specimens or as a group, as they come in various habits and sizes. Opt for small trees, preferably grafted maidens either bare root or container-grown.

GROWING TIP

Always prune established cherries in early or midsummer, to minimize the risk of infection from silver leaf or bacterial canker (see page 133), as these diseases are most infectious during the winter months and the pruning wounds are the likely entry point.

Family	Rosaceae
Height	5m/16ft
Spread	5m/16ft
Habit	Vase-shaped when young; spreading or weeping with maturity
Hardiness	Zone 6: −20 to −15°C/−4 to 5°F
Position	Full sun

OTHER NOTABLE SPECIES

- *P. sargentii* flowers in early spring on bare stems and is one of the first trees to develop autumnal colour (see also Five hardworking trees for any small garden, page 78).
- *P. × subhirtella* 'Autumnalis' (winter-flowering or autumn cherry) has small, semi-double, white flowers from autumn to spring.

HANAMI
This is the Japanese tradition of flower viewing – and in particular the *sakura* (cherry blossom). In modern-day Japan, *hanami* means picnicking beneath the canopies of cherry blossom trees during the day or night.

Willow-leaved pear

Pyrus salicifolia

From the Middle East comes the willow-leaved pear – a very popular, ornamental tree with a bushy crown, grown for its foliage and flowers. The leaves are pendent, silvery green, long and narrow, like a willow's (*Salix*), while the pure white flowers with black-tipped stamens appear in spring. The small fruits are hard and astringent and are not edible.

—

WHERE TO GROW

This tree will grow in any soil type providing it is moist but well-drained. It makes a good feature plant in a formal garden or border, especially if planted in front of an evergreen screen to show off the silver foliage.

HOW TO GROW

Buy a tree of 1.5m/5ft or less, as taller young trees will quickly become top-heavy and be a problem by falling over or leaning. If planted when small, the root system will keep up with the top growth and be able to support it.

GROWING TIP

The crown can become bushy and congested with crossing branches, but it can be difficult to open this up without the crown collapsing. Therefore, treat the crown like a piece of topiary and give the branch tips a regular clip back, to keep everything in check.

Family Rosaceae
Height 12m/40ft
Spread 6m/20ft
Habit Bushy or weeping
Hardiness Zone 6: –20 to –15°C/–4 to 5°F
Position Full sun

MERRY CHRISTMAS
A partridge in a pear tree was sent by the person's true love on the first day of Christmas in the English Christmas carol of 1780.

NOTABLE CULTIVAR AND ANOTHER NOTABLE SPECIES

- 'Pendula' is a weeping form of the species forming a congested top but showing off the silver foliage.
- *P. calleryana* 'Chanticleer' has a narrow crown with masses of white flowers and superb, fiery orange autumn colour.

Scarlet oak

Quercus coccinea

There are over 500 oak species from around the northern hemisphere, ranging from small, shrub-like trees to very large, wide-spreading ones living to a great age (see Researching and finding an old veteran tree, page 124). The scarlet oak is from Maine to Florida in the eastern USA, and it makes a large shade tree with deeply lobed leaves ending in bristle tips. They are a glossy dark green during summer, turning a bright scarlet in autumn (see also Making a collage of autumnal leaves in a picture frame, page 50). Some of the dead leaves remain on the tree well into winter.

—

WHERE TO GROW

Scarlet oak needs plenty of space to grow to its full potential and is not for the small garden. It prefers deep, fertile, well-drained, neutral to acidic soil and is not tolerant of alkaline conditions, unlike the English oak (*Q. robur*).

HOW TO GROW

Most of the oak species, including the scarlet oak, can be planted as small bare-root transplants or as field-grown or container-grown, semi-mature specimens. A good nurseryman will recommend the type of root system for the size of tree available for purchase at that nursery, as some can be difficult to transplant due to their taproots. See also Growing a tree from a seed, page 58.

GROWING TIP

This is a large shade tree and should be grown on a single trunk with its canopy and wide-spreading branches developing naturally.

Family Fagaceae

Height 20–25m/66–82ft

Spread 20m/66ft

Habit Rounded or open

Hardiness Zone 6: −20 to −15°C/−4 to 5°F

Position Full sun

NOTABLE CULTIVAR AND OTHER NOTABLE SPECIES

- 'Splendens' is even better than the species, with bright scarlet and crimson leaves in autumn.
- *Q. palustris* (pin oak) is fast-growing, has an open to spreading habit and is the easiest and most reliable oak tree to transplant. 'Green Pillar' is a columnar form of the species.
- *Q. rubra* (red oak) is a large tree, to 30m/100ft, with a spreading crown and large leaves turning red to brown before falling in autumn.

SCARLET FEVER

If you select the scarlet oak for your garden, you too on a sunny day in autumn will be able to enjoy the colours of the Appalachian Mountains in the USA, where this tree grows naturally.

Measuring a tree's height
and ageing it

The tallest tree in the world was discovered in 2006 and is a
coastal redwood (*Sequoia sempervirens*) in a secret location
in Redwood National and State Park. It is called Hyperion,
is estimated to be 600–800 years old and measures exactly
115.55m/379.1ft in height. To confirm the exact height,
these trees are actually climbed by skilled arborists and a
tape measure is dropped from the top to the ground and an
accurate measurement is taken. Finding such trees is exciting
and a challenge for the tree measurers in the difficult forested
locations that they grow in. Believe it or not, we are still
looking for a tree that may be taller still.

To climb to the top of a tall tree in a local park is not an
easy or safe option for many of us, but guessing the height
of trees and then verifying it by more accurate means are
fun. There are several ways to do this without the use of a
clinometer, which is an optical device for measuring elevation
angles above the horizontal.

One of the easiest ways to measure height is to use a piece
of paper and a little trigonometry. Fold a piece of square paper
in half to form a triangle, which will have one 90-degree right
angle and two 45-degree angles. Hold the triangle in front
of one eye by one of the 45-degree angle corners, with the
90-degree angle directly opposite, and look up the longest side
(the hypotenuse) by raising your eyes. Move backwards away
from the tree until you can see the top of the tree and continue
looking along the long length of the triangle until it comes in
line with the top of the tree. Mark this spot on the ground and
measure the distance to the base of the tree. This distance will
almost be the full height of the tree. Add your own height to
this measurement and you have the height of the tree.

To get a rough age of a tree, place a tape measure around
its trunk at 1.3m/4.3ft (roughly breast height) and for every
2.5cm/1in the tree gains another year of age, to within about
10 per cent.

1 Fold a piece of paper diagonally into a triangle.
2 Hold the triangle by the corner with the long length running at an angle.
3 Walk backwards until the top of the triangle is in line with the tree top (here, oak/*Quercus*).
4 Mark this spot and measure the distance to the tree. That length added to your own height is the height of the tree.

A Place a tape measure around the trunk of a tree (here, oak/*Quercus*) at breast height to measure its age.

Whitebeam

Sorbus aria

These are small to medium-sized trees with compact habits and young leaves emerging silvery white, before hardening off to green in summer. The clusters of creamy white flowers develop into orange-red fruits in autumn.

—

WHERE TO GROW

In its natural habitat this tree grows in calcareous soils on chalk downland and limestone cliffs, so needs a very free-draining, alkaline soil. With its silvery foliage, it makes the perfect solitary specimen tree in a small to medium-sized garden and will tolerate windy seaside conditions.

HOW TO GROW

These whitebeams grow and transplant well as a standard tree. Young trees have very thin bark, which bruises easily, so if staking is needed make sure you use a good-quality tree tie and buffer, to avoid rubbing.

GROWING TIP

Despite being a small tree, the branch attachments on whitebeam are very strong, and its wood is hard even for a pair of good-quality secateurs. Therefore, use a sharp, fine-toothed pruning saw of good-quality, instead of secateurs.

Family Rosaceae	
Height 8–12m/26–40ft	
Spread 4–8m/13–26ft	
Habit Columnar or rounded	
Hardiness Zone 6: –20 to –15°C/–4 to 5°F	
Position Full sun	

Sorbus aria

SHIPSHAPE BRISTOL FASHION
One of the rarest native trees in the UK is the Bristol whitebeam (*S. bristoliensis*), with only around one hundred growing on the cliffs in the Avon Gorge.

Sorbus alnifolia

Sorbus alnifolia

NOTABLE CULTIVARS AND OTHER NOTABLE SPECIES

- 'Lutescens' (silver-leaved whitebeam) has rounded leaves, which are covered in silver hairs on both sides.
- 'Magnifica' is a columnar tree, with large glossy leaves, cream flowers and red berries.
- 'Majestica' is a slower-growing whitebeam, with larger leaves than the species.
- *S. alnifolia* (Korean mountain ash) is a medium-sized tree with alder-like leaves, white flowers and persistent small, bright red berries.
- *S. intermedia* (Swedish whitebeam) develops a broad dense crown, and bears dark green, lobed leaves, white flowers and red berries.
- *S. thibetica* 'John Mitchell' is a columnar tree with an oval crown and large leaves displaying silver undersides.

Sorbus × intermedia

Rowan

Sorbus aucuparia aka mountain ash

This is a popular choice for a small garden. It has pinnate leaves, which develop good autumn colour (see also Making a collage of autumnal leaves in a picture frame, page 50), and clusters of creamy white flowers followed by orange-red berries in autumn. With its prolific flowering in spring and abundance of berries, rowan is a useful source of food for native and migratory birds, insects and bees.

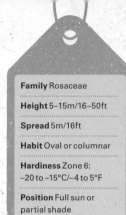

| Family Rosaceae |
| Height 5–15m/16–50ft |
| Spread 5m/16ft |
| Habit Oval or columnar |
| Hardiness Zone 6: –20 to –15°C/–4 to 5°F |
| Position Full sun or partial shade |

WHERE TO GROW

Rowans grow on well-drained, acid to neutral soils. Most make small trees, so are the perfect size for planting as specimen trees in a garden.

HOW TO GROW

These trees are available in a range of sizes – whips, feathered maidens, multi-stems and standards – and your final choice will depend on your budget and how long you are prepared to wait until it develops into a mature tree. Be aware that many of the cultivars are grafted on to a rootstock, so remove any suckers that appear below the graft union as early as possible (see Suckers and water shoots, page 43).

GROWING TIP

All of the rowans are prone to a disease called fireblight, which is caused by a bacterium *Erwinia amylovora* in late spring through to summer (see also page 135). It will eventually kill the tree. To minimize the risk of infection, it is is important to sterilize pruning tools between removing individual branches and between each tree.

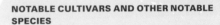

NOTABLE CULTIVARS AND OTHER NOTABLE SPECIES

There are many different species and cultivars available, so below are a few of the more popular ones with differing attributes.

- 'Aspleniifolia' has finely cut, fern-like leaves that develop good autumn colour, and it also carries orange-red berries.
- 'Sheerwater Seedling' is a fast-growing, columnar tree with large clusters of orange-red berries.
- *S. cashmiriana* is a native of Kashmir and has pink flowers followed by clusters of pearly white berries.
- S. 'Chinese Lace' is a small tree of columnar habit with deeply cut leaves giving a lace-like effect. .
- *S. commixta* 'Embley' is a small tree with a columnar habit, fiery-red autumn colour and masses of orange-red berries.
- S. 'Joseph Rock' is a beautiful small tree with a columnar habit and creamy yellow fruits.
- *S. pseudohupehensis* 'Pink Pagoda' is a really pretty rowan with blue-tinged leaves and clusters of pink fruits.
- *S. ulleungensis* has a columnar habit, creamy white flowers, fiery autumn foliage and orange berries (see also Five hardworking trees for any small garden, page 78).
- *S. vilmorinii* is a very well-behaved tree for the small garden, with delicate leaves and small berries in various shades of dark red to pinky white.

English yew

Taxus baccata

This medium-sized, long-lived evergreen conifer has been long associated with churchyards, druids and Christianity and is the oldest tree in Europe (see also Researching and finding an old veteran tree, page 124). Thin, flaking, reddish brown bark covers the main trunk and branches, which can be upright or spread horizontally. The leaves are linear green needles, which are poisonous if eaten – as are the seeds, which are enclosed by a bright translucent-red, berry-like fruit called an aril.

Family Taxaceae	
Height 3–8m/10–26ft	
Spread 3–8m/10–26ft	
Habit Rounded	
Hardiness Zone 7: <–20°C/–4°F	
Position Full sun or partial shade	

WHERE TO GROW

Yew is tolerant of most soils – alkaline or acid – providing they are well-drained; it dislikes waterlogging, which can ultimately lead to a fungal root rot called phytophthora (see page 135). It is a popular landscape tree in the garden. It also makes a good screen plant, a hedging one or topiary plant as it can be regularly pruned, making a tight face (see also Creating a standard topiary ball, page 110).

HOW TO GROW

This tree is readily available in a wide range of sizes from 20–100cm/8–39in transplants (which are bare-root) and 60–80cm/24–32in container-grown specimens to 1.25–2m/4–7ft root-balled plants. It is also possible to buy 100cm/39in lengths of established hedging in troughs from specialist nurseries.

GROWING TIP

As yew will not tolerate waterlogging or poor drainage, do not plant these trees too deep. Therefore, plant them slightly higher than the surrounding soil level, especially on clay soils.

NOTABLE CULTIVAR AND ANOTHER NOTABLE SPECIES

- 'Fastigiata' (Irish yew) has a very tight, columnar habit requiring no pruning; it adds formality to a garden.
- *T. brevifolia* (Pacific yew) is native to north-west North America, where it grows to 15m/50ft tall.

ANKERWYCKE YEW
This tree is thought to be some 2,000 years old, which means that it was over 1,000 years old when the British king John sealed the Magna Carta nearby, at Runnymede in 1215. It was also a secret meeting place for Henry VIII and Anne Boleyn.

Western red cedar

Thuja plicata

Western red cedar is a long-lived, fast-growing, very large tree in its native habitat on the west coast of North America, growing to a height of 70m/230ft, but is considerably smaller in cultivation. The foliage comprises glossy green, scale-like, weeping sprays turning bronze in winter and reverting to green again in summer. When cut or crushed, it smells of fresh pineapple.

Family Cupressaceae	
Height up to 35m/115ft	
Spread up to 9m/30ft	
Habit Pyramidal	
Hardiness Zone 6: −20 to −15°C/−4 to 5°F	
Position Full sun or partial shade	

WHERE TO GROW

This tree will grow in any moist or wet but free-draining soil. If sited in an open setting in a garden or park, it will retain its lower branches to the ground for many years, making an attractive specimen. It is also the perfect conifer for use as a formal hedging plant as it clips to shape well and forms a dense barrier in a screen.

ARBORVITAE
Despite its common name, *T. plicata* is not a true cedar (*Cedrus*) but an arborvitae, meaning 'tree of life'.

HOW TO GROW

For a single specimen, buy a root-balled or container-grown tree, which will mature into a large tree, but for hedging opt for smaller, bare-root transplants. After the first year but before it starts to get too leggy, start clipping the young tree, trimming only green foliage, not back to woody shoots.

GROWING TIP

To create a compact dense hedge of western red cedar, suitable spacing at planting time will be two or three plants per 1m/3ft length of hedge.

NOTABLE CULTIVAR AND ANOTHER NOTABLE SPECIES

- 'Atrovirens' has dense foliage, which makes it an excellent hedging plant.
- *T. occidentalis* (eastern white cedar) is commonly planted as an ornamental tree for screens and hedges; it is available in over 300 cultivars varying in shape, size and colour.

Researching and finding an old veteran tree

There is nothing more rewarding than discovering and meeting an old veteran tree and being able to witness the years and activities that it in turn has observed during its life cycle. Veteran trees can be found in a variety of places, such as rural parklands, commons, ancient woodlands and churchyards. But what is a veteran tree?

A veteran tree is not necessarily an ancient tree, but ancient trees are certainly veterans. It is difficult to clearly define, but a veteran tree is certainly a tree on its way to being ancient and is old in relation to other specimens of the same species. A veteran tree is interesting biologically and aesthetically, and has high amenity value and cultural or historic significance because of its age. It usually oozes character as it's well on its way to maturity, being hollowed out and gnarled by decay showing fungal fruiting bodies. It also might be stunted if it was a traditional pollard. In addition, such a veteran tree is of ecological importance to rare fungi, invertebrates, lichens, birds and bats by providing a habitat that younger trees are unable to offer.

To find an old veteran tree you need to do some homework and check out where such a tree may grow near you. There are several organizations online that will help you to find these amazing trees:

www.ancienttreeforum.co.uk/ ancient-trees/ ancient-tree- sites-to-visit

www.treeregister.org

www.ancient-yew.org

www.monumentaltrees.com

https://ati.woodlandtrust.org. uk/what-we-record-and-why/ what-we-record

THE CROWHURST YEW

This yew (*Taxus baccata*), which grows in the churchyard of St George's Church in Crowhurst, Surrey, UK, is estimated to be around 4,000 years old. It has so many stories to tell. During the nineteenth century, the Crowhurst yew was converted into a summer house with a table and chairs inside the hollow trunk, which could be entered through a small door in the side of the trunk. At this time, a cannon ball was discovered embedded in the trunk, dating back to the English Civil War in the seventeenth century.

Today it is an iconic tree for us all to enjoy, but please be careful when visiting veteran trees as they are fragile and suffer from compaction around the roots. Therefore, respect them and take away only photographs and memories.

A The Richmond Park 'Royal Oak' (*Quercus robur*), on the outskirts of London, UK, is said to be more than 750 years old.

B 'Big Lonely Doug' is a Douglas fir (*Pseudotsuga menziesii*) estimated to be between 750 and 1,200 years old; it grows near Port Renfrew on Vancouver Island, Canada.

C This 'Granny Scots Pine' (*Pinus sylvestris*), spotted in the Caledonian Forest, Scotland, is more than 300 years old.

D The California live oak (*Quercus agrifolia*) in the Jack London State Historic Park in California, USA, is believed to be more than 200 years old and is a magnificent evergreen specimen.

Small-leaved lime

Tilia cordata aka small-leaved linden

The small-leaved lime is a small to medium-sized tree with small, pale green, heart-shaped (cordate) leaves which are aphid free, so no honey dew is deposited. In midsummer, their clusters of small, sweetly scented flowers attract bees in great quantity. These flowers are attached to leafy green bracts, which develop into hanging groups of small round fruits while still retaining the leafy bracts, and act like parachutes during dispersal. Small-leaved lime is also a suitable host tree for growing mistletoe (see Establishing mistletoe in a garden tree, page 104).

—

WHERE TO GROW

All limes like to grow in deep, fertile, moist but well-drained, neutral to alkaline soil and are not tolerant of waterlogging. They like full sun and do not mind the heat of a hot summer providing they get some irrigation. The small-leaved lime makes a good avenue tree, as even seed-raised specimens generally have a uniform habit and shape.

HOW TO GROW

Most of the limes are available in many sizes, either field- or container-grown, and they are reliable when transplanted as large specimens. They make perfect freestanding specimens with well-balanced symmetrical crowns, and are also excellent for avenue planting. They can be planted in a row in the garden for pleaching (see page 43) and are also now readily available as pleached specimens in the garden centres and nurseries.

GROWING TIP

Look for a young nursery tree with healthy vigorous shoots and no algae or moss growing on the new stems. Moss and algae are signs that the young specimen lacks vigour and may well be stressed, which will reduce the success rate for establishment.

Family	Malvaceae
Height	17–25m/56–82ft
Spread	10m/33ft
Habit	Pyramidal when young; rounded in maturity
Hardiness	Zone 6: −20 to −15°C/−4 to 5°F
Position	Full sun

IT'S TEATIME
Tilleul (lime-blossom tea) is made from the infusion of the nectar-sweet flowers of the small-leaved lime and is a soothing and calming natural sleep aid.

NOTABLE CULTIVARS AND OTHER NOTABLE SPECIES

- 'Greenspire' is broadly pyramidal with ascending branches.
- 'Streetwise' makes a pyramidal form with ascending branches; it is suitable where space is at a premium.
- 'Winter Orange' is a striking, medium-sized tree bearing one- to two-year old twigs that are orange-red and highly ornamental in winter.
- *T. × europaea* (European lime) is the most commonly planted lime in the European landscape and gardens, and often produces lots of suckers at the base and in the lower crown.
- *T. henryana* is a choice species producing bronze-coloured young leaves with bristle tips.
- *T. tomentosa* (silver lime) has leaves that are green above and white beneath, and these are highlighted during summer when displayed in a breeze. 'Petiolaris' (weeping silver lime) is a graceful weeping form of the species.

Chusan palm

Trachycarpus fortunei

Trachycarpus is one of a few hardy palm trees that can be grown successfully in a temperate climate. Its large, evergreen, fan-shaped, palmate leaves are produced on long leaf stalks from hairy trunks. The Chusan palm is dioecious, with separate male and female plants. Small yellow flowers are borne on long pendulous panicles on trees of both sexes, but only the female plants go on to develop sprays of round black fruits.

—

WHERE TO GROW

This palm will grow in most soils from sand to clay, but they must be free-draining and never become waterlogged. Plant in a sheltered position in the garden, as strong winds can tear the large leaves. The Chusan palm makes a lovely solitary specimen, adding a tropical touch to the landscape despite it being a temperate palm.

HOW TO GROW

These palms are grown in containers in the nurseries, as they produce a mass of fibrous roots and so transplant better from a container. They are available in a multitude of sizes, usually with clear trunks but sometimes with multiple trunks arising from the base.

GROWING TIP

As the mature leaves turn yellow and hang down from the trunk, they can be removed close to the trunk with a sharp saw or secateurs, to tidy up the plant and at the same time raise the canopy.

Family	Arecaceae
Height	5m/16ft
Spread	1.5–2m/5–7ft
Habit	Vase
Hardiness	Zone 5: −15 to −10°C/5 to 14°F
Position	Full sun or partial shade

ANOTHER NOTABLE SPECIES

- *T. wagnerianus* is very similar to *T. fortunei*, except that it is slower-growing, and the leaves are smaller and stiffer, making them more suitable for windy sites.

PALM BEACH
This palm was introduced in 1849 from central China by Robert Fortune, after whom the species was named. Why not add an exotic feel to your garden by planting one?

Japanese zelkova

Zelkova serrata aka keaki

This zelkova is a medium to large, wide-spreading tree
making a beautiful, symmetrical, rounded crown with
smooth grey bark turning flaky with age and exposing
orange tints. The small, serrated, graceful leaves turn a
bronze-yellow-red colour in autumn before they eventually
fall (see also Making a collage of autumnal leaves in a
picture frame, page 50).

WHERE TO GROW

This tree needs a large garden to show off its wide-spreading
crown, but it can be planted in a container, which will restrict
its vigour and keep it small (see also Planting a tree in a pot for
a balcony, page 88). It will grow in any deep, acid or alkaline,
moist but well-drained soil in a sheltered spot and will tolerate
droughty conditions and air pollution once established.

HOW TO GROW

Plant a Japanese zelkova with a container-grown root system
or a root ball. It is available in a variety of sizes from 1m/3ft
to 7m/23ft tall, as a standard or multi-stemmed tree.

GROWING TIP

If planted as a small tree with a thin trunk, a Japanese zelkova
can be quite ungainly in its growth and form a bent trunk
from the weight of the crown. Therefore, tie the trunk to
a stout stake after planting, to ensure it grows straight –
unless you do not require that feature.

Family Ulmaceae

Height 10–18m/33–60ft

Spread 10m/33ft

Habit Vase when young;
rounded in maturity

Hardiness Zone 6:
–20 to –15°C/–4 to 5°F

Position Full sun or
partial shade

DUTCH ELM DISEASE
Although a member of
the elm family, Japanese
zelkova is resistant to
Dutch elm disease, making
it a good alternative
tree to elm (*Ulmus*) in a
landscape.

NOTABLE CULTIVARS AND ANOTHER
NOTABLE SPECIES

- Green Vase is a medium-sized, vase-shaped
  tree with attractive, bright green leaves in
  summer and showy autumnal colour.
- 'Village Green' is fast-growing, with a wide-
  spreading, vase-shaped crown.
- *Z. carpinifolia* (Caucasian elm) is a large shade
  tree with a short trunk and ascending branches.

Troubleshooting

'Trees are like people; they are moody, they stress, but they are beautiful when they are happy.'
(Tony Kirkham)

Growing trees is such a rewarding thing to do and will give you much pleasure and satisfaction. However, it is very disappointing when they succumb to pests and diseases or struggle to grow because of local environmental problems. As a tree grower, you need to be vigilant and observant through the seasons, keeping a lookout for these problems. Prevention is always better than cure, and you can minimize some of these problems by being proactive, carrying out good growing techniques, sound cultural methods and best practice when planting and pruning. Deal with trees that are showing signs of stress before they decline too far. There will often be a need to bring in a professional arborist for advice and help, but do not leave it too late (see When and how to hire a professional arborist, page 45).

The list of pests and diseases affecting ornamental trees is long, and sadly this list is growing annually as new ones turn up in gardens. Therefore, below are described some that are most common in gardens affecting trees. Also included are some cultural problems that may not yet have reached your part of the world, but you need to be aware of them and know what to look out for.

PESTS

Deer
These animals can cause browsing damage to new young growth, particularly young coppice shoots. A male deer will use a tree to remove velvet from his new antlers and mark his territory by rubbing his antlers on the trunks of young trees, removing strips of bark, disfiguring trees or girdling and eventually killing them. Control deer with fencing and by erecting guards around young trees.

Grey squirrels
Tree damage caused by grey squirrels is frequently seen on the branches and trunks of broadleaved trees of various ages and sizes, particularly oaks (*Quercus*), beeches (*Fagus*), maples (*Acer*) and hornbeam (*Carpinus*). It is caused by bark-stripping so the squirrel can drink the sap below. These branches can remain on the disfigured tree, ruining its shape, and will eventually die, becoming a safety issue should they break and fall.

Stripped bark damage on young tree trunks such as this willow (*Salix*) is caused by deer marking their territory with their antlers or removing velvet from their antlers.

Keep a vigilant look out for the early stages of leaf damage on a horse chestnut caused by the horse chestnut leaf miner.

The hairy caterpillars of the oak processionary moth are here feeding on English oak (*Quercus robur*) leaves.

Horse chestnut leaf miner
A common sight in late summer or early autumn is when all the leaves on a mature horse chestnut tree (*Aesculus hippocastanum*) turn brown and eventually fall off prematurely, causing the tree to stress and leaving it vulnerable to other pests and diseases. This disorder is caused by the larvae of a small moth, the leaf-mining moth (*Cameraria ohridella*), which bores between the upper and lower surfaces of the leaves, eating the chlorophyll. To control it, rake up the fallen leaves and burn them because the moth overwinters as eggs in the old leaves.

Oak processionary moth (OPM)
OPM (*Thaumetopoea processionea*) is a pest of several European oak (*Quercus*) species and was first accidentally introduced into the UK on imported oak trees in 2005. The larvae of the moth feeds on the leaves of oak trees, leaving skeletonized leaves. During its life cycle, OPM sheds its skin and hairs six times, eventually pupating in a nest on the trunk or main branches of the tree, which it makes from silk and old hairs. The moth emerges in summer and lays its eggs in plaques on the small, pencil-thin twigs in the upper part of the canopy. If discovered, do not touch the caterpillars as the

hairs are toxic. Always seek advice from professional arborists (see When and how to hire a professional arborist, page 45). Control is essential by the use of pesticides.

Pine processionary moth (PPM)
This insect pest (*Thaumetopoea pityocampa*) is moving across Europe and has currently reached Paris, so we must be vigilant and prevent it from infecting any more pine trees. Watch out for signs of its symptomatic silky nests, defoliated branches and processions of hairy caterpillars.

Stem- and trunk-boring insects
There are several of these insect pests that will attack trees. Some of them are not yet in the UK, but they are established in northern Europe and the USA. They include emerald ash borer, bronze birch borer, Asian and citrus longhorn beetles and ambrosia beetles. Identification is usually by discovering tree frass (sawdust) from their boring activity around entry holes on the trunk. Branches with boring damage that become hazardous can be removed and burned, and multi-stemmed trees of susceptible tree species can be grown so that infected trunks can be removed without the loss of the entire tree. If in doubt call in a professional arborist (see When and how to hire a professional arborist, page 45).

DISEASES

Anthracnose of plane
This is a disease affecting young and mature plane (*Platanus*) trees including the London plane (*P. × hispanica*),

and it can vary in severity from year to year depending on rainfall and temperatures. The classic symptom is leaf wilt resembling frost damage (see page 136) followed by premature leaf fall in early summer. The only real control is to collect and burn fallen leaves, as most healthy trees will grow out of anthracnose without too many problems because the tree has learnt to live with it.

Ash dieback
Also known as Chalara dieback, this fungal disease is having a devastating effect on all ash trees of all ages. However, young trees are quicker to succumb to it than older specimens, showing the symptoms early and dying quickly. The leaves wilt and turn black, the shoots wither and dark diamond lesions develop on the trunk where the small lateral branches join it. Eventually, as the disease develops in a mature tree, it starts to produce lots of dead wood and dies back from the tips of the canopy. There is no control, so replace it with one from a different genus.

Bacterial canker of cherry
Bacterial canker is a disease caused by two bacteria infecting the stems and leaves of fruit trees and ornamental flowering cherries and other *Prunus* species. The symptoms on the stems and trunk are dead areas of bark with a sticky gum oozing from it. This is followed by wilting and dieback of the new shoots (not to be confused with the fungal disease blossom wilt) or shoots failing to develop. Small brown spots appear,

A sticky gum oozing from the trunk of cherry (*Prunus*) trees is a typical symptom of bacterial canker of cherry, followed by wilting leaves and ultimately death on young trees.

Ganoderma applanatum, which is nicknamed the artist's fungi, is a common decay bracket fungus on broadleaved trees.

eventually leaving holes in the leaves; this is known as 'shot hole'. There is no chemical control, so prevention is the only course of action. Carry out any pruning in summer, when the disease is dormant. Prune back beyond any infected areas, sterilizing pruning tools between cuts to prevent infecting healthy parts of the tree and to stop transmission between trees.

Decay fungi

Wood-decaying fungi are some of the most common types of tree diseases. Before you can determine the extent of the decay and the weakness of the wood structure in a tree, which

can ultimately lead to tree failure, you need to discover the type and species of the fungi, that is whether it is a brown rot, a white rot or a soft rot. There are many species of wood-decay fungi that feed on moist wood, causing it to rot, but most of them produce a bracket fungus on the trunk or main branches during autumn, which will help to identify the disease. It is important to seek professional advice from a qualified arborist and remember that a hollow tree can still be very strong (see When and how to hire a professional arborist, page 45).

Honey fungus is the killer fungus on tree roots that we all dread seeing in our gardens. Immediately remove the affected tree and all its roots.

Honey fungus

This is a very destructive parasitic fungal disease caused mainly by the fungus *Armillaria mellea*, which spreads underground and feeds on tree roots. The tree generally looks unhealthy and produces fewer and smaller leaves than previously; branches die back and there is rot at the base of the trunk, where it meets the soil. Eventually, the whole tree will die. In autumn, small, honey-coloured mushrooms can be seen growing at the base of the tree. There are no chemicals to treat honey fungus, so keeping trees healthy and stress-free and removing infected trees with their infected roots are the main means of control.

Leaf rust

This is more of an eyesore that is harmless, and it rarely kills trees. However, it can weaken trees by reducing their ability to photosynthesize and it does leave them open to other infections. Bright orange or red spots appear on the leaves, followed by the leaves curling up and eventually falling off. There are several fungicides available in garden centres, which can be applied to small trees, but maintaining a healthy tree and collecting leaves and burning them will help to control leaf rust.

Fireblight

This disease, *Erwinia amylovora*, is most commonly found on fruit trees and ornamental trees in the rose family, Rosaceae. The first signs of fireblight are wilting leaves in spring in warm humid weather during the flowering period; the leaves eventually turn black sporadically through the crown. If a twig is cut with secateurs, there could be staining in the wood. To control fireblight, prune out infected branches back to uninfected wood. Always sterilize pruning tools between pruning cuts to prevent spreading the disease.

Phytophthora root rot

This is a fungal disease that attacks trees growing on poorly drained, waterlogged soils and causes a root rot. The symptoms are similar to a tree suffering from drought stress, that is the leaves wilt and eventually turn yellow. There is no treatment, so prevention is important: for example, avoid planting trees on wet soils with no drainage; select more suitable tree species for a damp spot; and do not overwater during dry spells. Trees planted too deep – that is, above the nursery mark – will also be affected by root rot.

Powdery mildew

A powdery white covering on leaves is the symptom of a fungal disease known as powdery mildew. The leaves eventually become distorted, turn yellow and fall off prematurely. Powdery mildew is caused when humidity is high and there is little air circulation through trees in shady parts of a garden. Fungicides can be applied, but it is better to improve air circulation.

Xylella

Currently in Mediterranean regions is found the bacterium *Xylella fastidiosa*, which can cause a devastating disease on a wide range of broadleaved trees. The symptoms are very similar to those of drought (see right), frost damage (see right) or a wilt disease, and confirmation that the problem is *Xylella* will involve tests in a laboratory. High-risk trees include olives (*Olea*) as well as cherries, plums and almonds (all *Prunus*), but most broadleaved trees can play host to this disease. Strict biosecurity is key to success, so this disease is not introduced into new areas. Therefore, do not be tempted to bring plants or cuttings home from overseas holidays and where possible buy locally sourced and grown trees from your local nursery industry.

ENVIRONMENTAL PROBLEMS

Compacted soils

Tree roots are generally shallow and as we walk or drive over the root plate of a tree we add to the compaction, reducing air movement, gaseous exchange and water percolation to the root zone. This stresses trees of any age – from young to mature – and reduces root activity and root growth. The tree will go into decline, producing dieback and dead wood in the canopy, eventually leading to death. This can be rectified by loosening the soil around the root plate and by mulching with organic matter to prevent further re-compaction.

Drought

One of the most common reasons for young trees failing to establish after tree planting is lack of water during dry periods. It can take twelve months for a tree to potentially die if it is not watered. The symptoms are basically a stressed-looking tree with wilting and yellowing leaves, leading to premature leaf drop. If the shrivelled leaves remain on the tree, then this is a bad sign and the tree has most likely died. To prevent such a problem, water young trees regularly during dry periods, before they start to show signs of stress, and seal in the water with an application of mulch around the base.

Frost damage

Frost damage affects the tender new shoots and flowers of trees in late spring, particularly of walnuts (*Juglans*), katsura trees (*Cercidiphyllum japonicum*) and other tender tree

An apparent dusting of talcum powder over the leaves of an English oak (*Quercus robur*) is the classic symptom of powdery mildew.

Wilting and browning of leaves on this walnut (*Juglans regia*) indicate frost damage and are likely to occur on young trees after a late spring frost.

species with fleshy shoots in spring. The new shoots or leaves wilt and quickly turn brown or black, crisping and eventually falling off. Providing the tree is established and healthy, it will send out new growth and mature out of the damage. During prolonged periods of frost, roots can be damaged, especially when grown on wet or waterlogged soils. Also during very frosty weather the leaves of evergreens can be scorched by wind. Avoid planting tender plants in frost pockets and cover tender plants with some form of protection such as fleece if frosts are forecast.

Herbicide damage

Most gardeners want a lawn that is weed-free and a lush green, even during periods of drought. However, lawn weed and feed products that are applied to lawns can seep through to the root zone of nearby trees, which then take the herbicide up into the leaves. When applied during hot weather, the chemicals can evaporate and rise up into the branches of overhanging trees, distorting or killing the foliage. Avoid the use of such weedkillers or follow the recommended dilution rates, and never apply them in hot weather.

Lawnmower and strimmer damage

When a lawnmower or other machine knocks against a tree trunk, or a strimmer cord comes into contact with the bark at the root collar, it bruises the bark and permanently damages the layers of cells beneath the bark. This causes dead tissue and provides an entry point for infection; it also restricts the flow of water and nutrients up the trunk. If the trunk is girdled, the tree will die. To avoid such damage, maintain a grass- or weed-free area around the base of each tree so machinery is kept well away.

Nutrient deficiency

As gardeners we are far too clean and tidy in our gardens, annually raking up leaves off the lawn and in the flower borders as they fall, leading to hungry trees. In nature, trees feed on the leaves, fruits and small twigs that fall and decompose. We can help by leaving mulched circles around our trees and blowing the dead leaves on to these mulched zones, mimicking a woodland floor and replenishing the soil with nutrients. The trees will thank you for it.

Soil build-up over tree roots

During the construction of new houses or hard landscape projects in the garden, soil levels can be built up over root plates and around trunks above the root crowns. This can have an adverse effect on the tree as the roots have developed over time to the original soil levels. Therefore, you should lower the soil level over such sensitive places, although you may still find damage has already been done.

Trees planted too deep

If some form of support like a tree stake is still needed two or three years after a tree has been planted, because the roots continue to move in the ground when the tree is rocked, and a space opens up around the base of the tree, it is probable that the tree was planted too deeply. This will eventually kill the tree, or it will fail to establish. If the tree is young enough and still has some vigour, it can be replanted at the correct depth (see Planting a tree, page 24). Otherwise, you will need to start again and plant a new tree at the correct planting depth.

Tree-staking damage

Often tree stakes and ties are left on a tree for too long after tree planting, and if not adjusted during the growing season they can cut into the tree, or the stake can chafe on the trunk, causing irreparable bark wounds. Therefore, ensure that stakes and ties are removed as soon as the tree is stable, to prevent this type of damage. See also Checking supports, page 30.

A clean, weed-free, mulched circle around each tree is one of the best ways to keep trees healthy and well fed, and it looks good in the garden, too.

What to do when

Trees are generally low-maintenance once established and independent, but to get the best out of the trees in your garden there will always be the occasional job to do.

SPRING

- Water newly planted trees, especially during dry weather, and also check – and if necessary water – trees planted in the last five years.
- Check tree ties on newly planted trees and adjust where needed (see page 30; also Tree-staking damage, page 139).
- Carry out formative pruning on young trees (see page 42).
- Water trees in pots regularly to prevent them from drying out.
- Repot trees planted in containers that have become pot-bound (see Planting a tree in a pot for a balcony, page 88).
- Feed trees in pots with a well-balanced fertilizer (see Feeding, page 30).
- Check for pests and diseases on all trees in the garden and take appropriate action (see Troubleshooting, page 130).
- Plant trees if the autumn planting season has been missed (see Planting a tree, page 24).
- Take softwood cuttings (see page 32).
- Check for obvious defects in mature trees following adverse weather such as strong winds (see Responsibilities of tree owners, page 34).

- Arrange a health check of the trees in the garden from an experienced arborist (see When and how to hire a professional arborist, page 45).

SUMMER

- Water newly planted trees during droughty weather.
- Summer-prune *Prunus* species to avoid infection from silver leaf disease or bacterial canker (see page 133).
- Summer-prune tree species that bleed sap (see When is the best time to prune trees?, page 38).
- Prune out suckers from the rootstocks of grafted trees (see Suckers and water shoots, page 43).
- Remove dead wood from trees while it is easy to spot against the live branches (see How to prune trees, page 39).
- Take some time out to visit gardens and arboreta to see trees that may be the next one you decide to plant in your garden.
- Contact a tree nursery or garden centre and place an order for the purchase of new trees in preparation for autumn/ winter planting (see Buying a tree, page 20).
- Take semi-ripe cuttings of conifers (see page 32).

AUTUMN

This is the start of the tree-planting season. Those planted now will benefit by being partly established by spring, when there is a high possibility of periods of drought.

- After planting a tree, give it a good mulch (see Mulching trees, page 29).
- Collect any seeds from trees and sow them (see page 30). See also Growing a tree from a seed, page 58.
- Autumn is the time to check out your trees for decay fungi (see page 134), which will start to produce fruiting bodies now.
- Rake up leaves of trees with pests and diseases, and dispose of them by burning or composting to eliminate the pests and diseases.
- Once young trees are established, remove tree stakes (see Checking supports, page 30).
- Collect and press leaves with autumn colour (see Making a collage of autumnal leaves in a picture frame, page 50).

WINTER

- Plant bare-root nursery stock (see Planting a tree, page 24).
- Continue planting container-grown trees into winter if additional planting time is needed.
- Clean tree circles of weeds and top up with organic mulch (see Mulching trees, page 29).
- Rake up fallen leaves and make compost with them. They can then be added to the tree circles once fully decomposed.
- Take hardwood cuttings of your favourite broadleaved trees and set them in a free-draining potting compost (see page 31).
- Carry out any tree pruning during the dormant period, especially trees that bleed sap (see Pruning trees, page 34).

Index

Brimming with creative inspiration, how-to projects and useful information to enrich your everyday life, Quarto Knows is a favourite destination for those pursuing their interests and passions. Visit our site and dig deeper with our books into your area of interest: Quarto Creates, Quarto Cooks, Quarto Homes, Quarto Lives, Quarto Drives, Quarto Explores, Quarto Gifts, or Quarto Kids.

First published in 2021 by Frances Lincoln,
an imprint of The Quarto Group.
The Old Brewery, 6 Blundell Street
London, N7 9BH,
United Kingdom
T (0)20 7700 6700 F (0)20 7700 8066
www.QuartoKnows.com

Text © 2021 Tony Kirkham
Photographs © 2021 Tony Kirkham
Illustrations © the Board of Trustees of the Royal Botanic
Gardens, Kew, unless otherwise stated

A catalogue record for this book is available from the British Library.

ISBN 978-0-7112-6198-3

10 9 8 7 6 5 4 3 2 1

Typeset in Stempel Garamond and Univers
Design by Glenn Howard

Printed in China

Dedicated to my mother

Picture acknowledgements

Asako Kuwajima: 113

GAP Photos: 20 left (Friedrich Strauss); 89 below right (Friedrich Strauss)

Getty Images: 126 (Nastasic)

Metropolitan Museum of Art: 83 below (Purchase, The Annenberg Foundation Gift, 1993)

Shutterstock: 13 above (kareemov1000); 13 below (Jollanda); 106 (Viktoriia Janis)

Wellcome Collection: 81 above right (Public Domain)